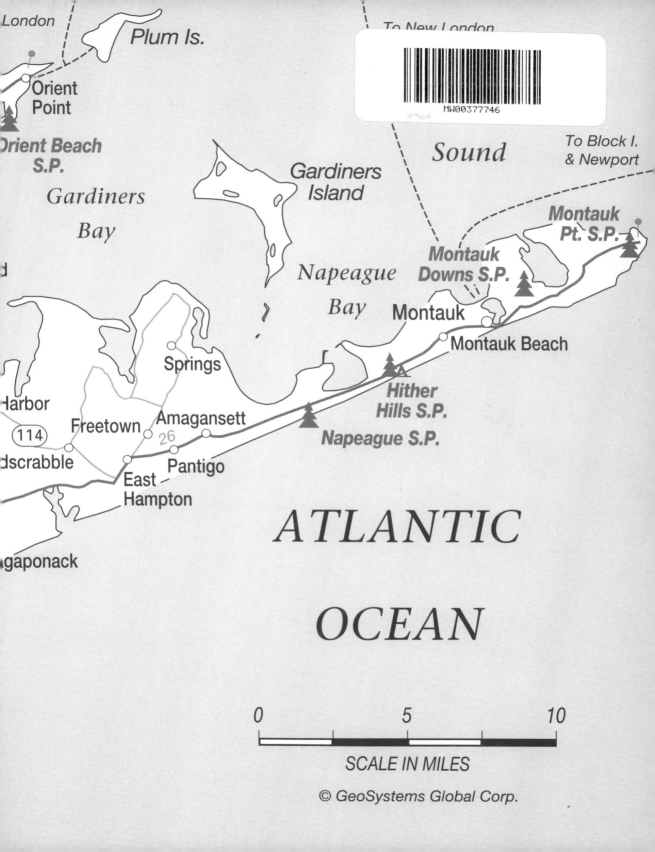

London

Plum Is.

To New London

Orient
Point

Sound

To Block I.
& Newport

Orient Beach
S.P.

Gardiners
Island

Montauk
Pt. S.P.

Gardiners
Bay

Montauk
Downs S.P.

Napeague
Bay

Montauk

Montauk Beach

Springs

Hither
Hills S.P.

Harbor

Freetown

Amagansett

Napeague S.P.

(114)

26

dscrabble

Pantigo

East
Hampton

ATLANTIC

gaponack

OCEAN

0   5   10

SCALE IN MILES

© GeoSystems Global Corp.

Tasting The Hamptons

FOOD, POETRY AND ART FROM LONG ISLAND'S EAST END

Katherine Hartnett

Foreword by
Richard Scholem, New York Times

Mill House Inn
Bed and Breakfast
33 North Main Street
East Hampton, NY 11937

(516) 324-9766

www.millhouseinn.com

First Printing   3,000   July, 1998

ISBN 0-9663959-0-5

Printed in the USA by

WIMMER
The Wimmer Companies
Memphis

Acknowledgments

This book could not have been born without the effort and creative talents of many people.

Thank you to Robin Goldfarb, the manager of the Mill House Inn, for all of the endless typing, proofreading and a thousand other things to make it happen. To Lori Banks Hurley, the Mill House Inn chef for committing our recipes to paper. To Gail Greco for her support, encouragement, invaluable expertise and editing throughout this long process.

Thank you also to Hugh King, Scott Chaskey, Jackie Little, Kathy Lynaugh and Stanley Bell for contributing your artistic talents.

A special thank you to Robert Fairbrother the General Manager of the Laundry Restaurant and President of the Long Island Chapter of the Sommelier Society of America, and Michelle Napoli, Assistant Managing Editor, with the East Hampton Star for contributing the material for the Wineries chapter at the eleventh hour.

To Steve Haweeli of Wordhampton, Public Relations for letting me keep talking and encouraging me to keep going.

To my friend Barbara Brass for all of her creative wisdom and for giving me the key to getting this done.

And last and most important thank you to my husband Dan and my children Brook, Sean and Denis for being there and loving me.

Table of Contents

Foreword

Richard Jay Scholem, New York Times

The Hamptons have it all; they are a chef's dream. The restaurants of the East End are surrounded by an unrivaled bounty of the land and sea. Long Island ducks and potatoes are known and requested by discerning restaurateurs around the world. Strawberries, tomatoes and pumpkins mark the seasons and fill the East End's fields. The waters of the Atlantic Ocean, Peconic Bay and Long Island Sound yield a continuing harvest of lobster, scallops, crabs, oysters, clams, tuna, striped bass, bluefish and literally dozens of other sea creatures. An ever increasing profusion of grapes flourish on the North Fork. They are made into the cabernet sauvignon, merlot, cabernet franc, chardonnay, sauvignon blanc and reisling wines served not only on the East End, but in the restaurants of Manhattan, London and even Paris.

This cornucopia, this avalanche remained largely untapped until a decade or so ago. Then some enterprising entrepreneurs figured out how to provide year round, rather than seasonal employment for East End chefs. After the Hamptons season ended they moved the chefs to restaurants they owned in Manhattan, Florida and the Caribbean. Their initiative attracted some of this nation's and Europe's most talented chefs to the tip of Long Island. The result of this restaurant revolution is a 60 mile stretch that boasts more talented chefs, great restaurants and local agricultural products than any area of the country other than perhaps Manhattan. Add a discerning, discriminating clientele with sophisticated palates and the wealth and inclination to sample great food and you have a golden, promised land for diverse restaurants and great chefs.

Now the Mill House Inn, an exquisite gem of a bed and breakfast in East Hampton, is presenting this cookbook, enriched with local art, photography and poetry and featuring the most outstanding dishes the restaurants of the Hamptons have to offer. Along with the recipes for saffron risotto with asparagus and mussels from Nick and Toni's, the roast swordfish with red lentil crust from Caswells and oysters on the half shell with ginger mignonette granite from Alison by the Beach, you will also find dishes from the Mill House Inn's fabled breakfasts. Good reading, good eating, bon appetit.

Richard Jay Scholem, a restaurant critic and columnist, writes the "A La Carte" column in the <u>New York Times'</u> Long Island edition.

Introduction

The "Hamptons" which consists roughly of the area between Westhampton and Montauk at the eastern end of Long Island in New York, is an area of unparalleled natural beauty. Over the course of its 350 year history, it has attracted settlers looking for a promised land of religious freedom and prosperity; artists drawn by the incredible vistas and natural light and tourists looking for the pleasures of the world's most spectacular beaches. Most recently, the area has become a magnet for fine restaurants, professional theater and film and increasingly more prestigious wineries.

This book, a labor of love for its many contributors, is an effort to celebrate the richness and beauty of this land through food, poetry and art. East Hampton towncrier and history buff, Hugh King has generously shared his wealth of knowledge about East Hampton's early beginnings in helping to compile a brief historical essay. We have divided the following chapters into seven main sections. The first four contain breakfast recipes from the Mill House Inn, in a seasonal format reflecting our approach to preparing food for our guests. These are followed by a selection of recipes featuring some of our finest restaurants and chefs who have contributed recipes for their favorite entrées.

We follow these with a chapter featuring Long Island wines. In the past twenty-five years, the East End, particularly the North Fork, has gradually reinvented itself from primarily producing the world famous Long Island potato and duckling to growing and producing increasingly important Long Island wines. As wine is often the perfect accompaniment to a fine meal, we drew upon the expertise of Robert Fairbrother, General Manager of **The Laundry Restaurant** in East Hampton and President of the Long Island Chapter of the Sommelier Society of America and Michelle Napoli, a native of East Hampton and Assistant Managing Editor of <u>The East Hampton Star</u> to talk about winemaking on the East End and successfully pairing wines with foods.

Finally, there is a chapter of easy and delicious hors d'oeuvre recipes drawn from our "Cooking Classes in the Hamptons" series, held during the summer and autumn months at the Mill House Inn.

It has also been a pleasure to welcome the talents of several local artists. Our poet, Scott Chaskey, is the head farmer at Quail Hill Farm, an organic farm in Amagansett. His poems, which introduce the breakfast chapters, take us around the seasons through the eyes of a man intimately connected to the land. Artist Jacqueline Toale Little, has taken the images Scott created with words and fashioned them into a series of pen and ink drawings, reflecting the beauty of the land around her. The photographs, contributed by Kathy Lynaugh of Montauk, and Stanley Bell of East Hampton, highlight the natural beauty of our area and the stunning still-lives created by the foods contributed by our chefs.

Those of us who worked together to create this book are all drawn to the East End by the same forces that brought the earliest settlers and the most recent visitors. We love the blending of farm land and beaches, local wineries and local fishing. We appreciate the abundance of artistic talent and fine foods that exist in a picturesque rural setting. We welcome the opportunity to raise our children in this land as so many generations of settlers have before us. It is all that and more that we celebrate in this book, <u>Tasting the Hamptons</u>.

If you haven't visited eastern Long Island yet, we invite you to taste the best of the Hamptons through the pages of this book. If you know the area, sit back and savor again the beauty you know so well and sample some of the fine regional foods captured in our recipes.

Katherine Hartnett
East Hampton, New York
March, 1998

Who They Were and How They Lived: A Taste of Local History

Compiled by Hugh King, East Hampton Town Crier

Of the original nine settlers who founded East Hampton in 1648, six migrated from an early settlement in Lynn, Massachusetts. Others came from nearby Southampton and other early settlers in East Hampton can be traced to Maidstone, Kent in England. Since the early settlers were English, they maintained strong social and economic ties with the New England colonies and with England.

The governors of the New Haven and Connecticut colonies, Theophilus Easton and Edward Hopkins purchased about 30,000 acres of land from the Montaukett Indians, the native inhabitants of Eastern Long Island, in 1648. An additional 10,000 acres were acquired sometime between 1658 and 1686.

The Montauketts, part of the Algonquin nation, did not realize that they were selling their land forever, as native Americans did not have the same concept of land ownership as the European settlers. The tribe was effectively shut out from continuing their long established traditions of hunting and gathering for food.

The Europeans also introduced diseases for which the Montauketts possessed no immunity and thus their numbers dwindled rapidly and by 1840 there were only six families, numbering about thirty people left.

While reasons for moving to a hazardous new settlement in the wilderness of Eastern Long Island are not clear, we can make some educated guesses as to why. It may be that the English governors in the New World encouraged the settlement in order to forestall the Dutch who also had their eyes on acquiring Eastern Long Island.

Happy people don't migrate and many may have been dissatisfied with their lot and hoped for a new start in East Hampton. Since many had emigrated from Kent in England, an area not dissimilar to East Hampton, the farming skills and knowledge of sea and ships possessed by the early settlers fit well within the natural advantages offered by Eastern Long Island. When the earliest settlers arrived, they found a bountiful supply of fertile ground, game and fish available to them.

The first inhabitants of East Hampton built their cottages in what is now the southern end of Main Street on either side of the marsh which is now Town Pond. The first town dwellings were hardly more than rude shelters, cellars dug in the ground, the walls covered with timber and roofed with thatch.

In time the settlers began to erect the typical new England style salt-box houses some twenty-five feet high in front sloping to about eight feet in the rear. The Mulford House and Home Sweet Home house survive on the south end of Main Street as classic examples of these first houses. The great width of Main Street in East Hampton is due to the fact that the road was used as a thoroughfare for sheep and cattle to be driven to the pasture in Montauk.

Soon after the settlement was established, the townsmen built a network of roads through the surrounding wilderness. A port was established in Northwest and remained until Sag Harbor was settled in 1730. Other roads were cleared to the salt meadow at Accabonac and in Springs and Napeague, and to the grazing lands in Wainscott and Montauk. The settlement spread out within a few years much to its present boundaries.

By the time the port of Sag Harbor was established, East Hampton was able to export to the West Indies and other markets the local products of hides, beef, tallow, pork, hoops, cattle, horses, fish, shoes, candles, oats, corn and other grains.

But the real economic boom to early East Hampton occurred with the discovery of the value of whales. In the late 1670's the townsmen began to hunt and kill the whales instead of waiting for them to wash up accidentally on the shore. In this way, they discovered a means of paying for all of the manufactured items that they imported from England, New York, Boston and the West Indies. Whales contributed greatly to the town's prosperity with shipments of sperm whales, oil and whalebones a source of much capital.

By the middle of the eighteenth century, the first of three successive generations of the Dominy family began making the furniture, clocks and windmills for which they are famous, on the family property, formally located on North Main Street in what is now a public parking lot.

Soon the settlers began building sawmills and gristmills turned by horses and bullocks. Later they were replaced by "petticoat" or "smock" windmills, so called because of the shape of their rotating caps which could turn to catch a favorable wind. The Hook Mill, located across the street from the Mill House Inn, on North Main Street was built in 1806 by Nathanial Dominy as an excellent example of this type of windmill.

Until the coming of the Long Island Railroad at the end of the nineteenth century, the farming economy in East Hampton was primarily of a subsistence nature with the residents producing or hunting all of the foodstuffs which they consumed.

> "The main foods consisted of venison, wild birds, fish and clams, with pumpkin, corn and wild greens for vegetables. Bread was mostly corn or rye; cornmeal called "injin" (Indian) meal was made into a pudding topped off with West Indies molasses. The fruits were wild-wild strawberries, blackcap, raspberries, blackberries, blueberries and beachplums. In the fall there were big purple wild grapes from Montauk and cranberries from low marshy spots between the sand dunes in Napeague."[3]

Although East Hampton had always enjoyed a commerce relationship with various ports, when the railroad arrived, East Hampton's fairly self contained existence of 250 years changed. Its development as a resort area began and the nature of its farming and trading evolved as well.

Due to the fertile soil and long growing season, East Hampton became able to develop cash crops in addition to those used to feed her population. The best known of these is the potato which soon became the main source of income for East Hampton farmers.

Faster transportation to the city also allowed for the development of a large scale commercial fishing industry. Cod, sturgeon and its roe, clams and the delectable bay scallop all of which were plentiful in those days became sources of profit well into the present century. Today East Hampton's popularity as a resort continues to increase.

The present day economy is based largely on tourism with the completion of the Long Island Expressway and the extension of the Sunrise Highway. As the population increases we appreciate and value more and more the stunning natural beauty of the area and what remains of East Hampton's long and prosperous agricultural history. We invite you to do the same.

Sources:

1. Breen, T.H. Imagining the Past. Addison-Wesley Publishing Company: New York, 1989.

2. Epstein, Jason and Elizabeth Barlow. East Hampton: A History and Guide. Medway Publishing: Sag Harbor, NY, 1975.

3. Rattray, Jeannette Edwards. East Hampton History: Including Geneologies of Early Families. East Hampton, NY, 1953.

About the Mill House Inn

The history of the building which is now the Mill House Inn, has always been closely connected to the agricultural heritage of East Hampton. Built in the 1790's by the Parsons family, one of East Hampton's original settlers, the Mill House has played its part in local history. The Parsons family at one time owned and farmed enormous tracts of land employing many seasonal farm workers. In 1860 the house was sold to Patrick Lynch, a Parsons farm employee. Lynch had arrived in East Hampton as an Irish immigrant, shipwrecked in Amagansett as he fled Ireland's great potato famine.

At various times the house served different functions. During the 1880's the house was a temporary Catholic church while the village's present church was being constructed. It was later the site of a local butcher shop in addition to remaining the Lynch family home until the 1970's.

Today the Mill House Inn is an eight room bed and breakfast located in the heart of East Hampton village. Throughout its history, the Mill House has had a nearly continuous tradition of housing visitors to the East End of Long Island, first as a boarding house for summer visitors and farm workers and then as a guest house until the late 1980's. Most recently, we have fully renovated and refurbished the rooms adding such amenities as fireplaces and whirlpool baths in the guest rooms and completely redecorating the public areas. As we discovered more about the house's rich history, we became more committed to peeling off the layers of time and restoring the house to its original beauty. We hope our work reflects a gentle co-mingling of the past with the best of today's comforts.

At the Mill House, we offer our guests the personal attention and hospitality of a small inn as well as some extra luxuries that make their visit a little more relaxing and a little more special. We are especially proud of our full gourmet breakfast featuring delicious homecooked entrées and freshly baked breads and muffins. Visitors are also treated to an afternoon snack of sweet treats served in the dining room with hot tea in the fall and winter or iced tea and lemonade in the summer.

Our sunny front porch with white rockers and french doors makes the perfect setting for enjoying a refreshing drink and is often the site of festive cocktail parties throughout the summer. In the cooler months, our guests retire to the inn living room, where a crackling fire in the fireplace and several cozy sitting areas entice them to enjoy a book, a game or a conversation with a cup of tea.

In the pages that follow, we offer you a sample of the best of our breakfast recipes, presented in menus reflecting the four seasons. Living in what is still today an agricultural community, we strive to treat our guests to the best ingredients that each season has to offer. In the spring and early summer we welcome the first rhubarb and the juiciest local strawberries. As the summer reaches its peak we pick the ripest tomatoes, fresh basil and cilantro to add to our frittatas and mint to accent the many succulent fruits available to us locally. Throughout the autumn and winter we enjoy the abundance of potatoes, pumpkins and cranberries, using them in a variety of ways in our breakfast menus. We hope you enjoy preparing and serving these meals to your guests as much as we do to ours.

Spring

3-Mile Harbor Inlet in the Springs

Primavera

At the open door I cradle my daughter

facing bay backwater. March light

filters silver on beak, wing, feather

of white and black buffleheads,

iridescent mallard

the snow swans,

and on kingfisher's crown.

Sun is an hourglass shape

on the instrument of water- reflected

starlight crossed by kingfisher's rattle,

duck's slide - and completely Spring - like

diamond spin in the wise liquid of my daughter's eye.

–Scott Chaskey

Springtime, A Season of Renewal

After the sleepy East End winter, we eagerly look forward to the joys of Spring. Come out and visit us and enjoy the gentle pleasures of this "shoulder season". The many nurseries and florists are overflowing with spring flowers and plants and we anticipate the fun of planting our gardens. Plan a day trip out to the North or South Fork and browse the nurseries filled with a colorful array of pansies, hyacinths and other early flowers in addition to outdoor sculpture and furnishings.

Our fisherman friends enjoy the annual run of cod and flounder, abundantly available in Lake Montauk. The Lazy Bones Fishing Boats (516-668-5671) have great day trips into the calm, sheltered waters. Their motto is "bring your lunch, catch your dinner". It is a fun outing with children- but don't forget to dress warmly, the winds can still be chilly.

In early Spring, don't miss the Montauk St. Patrick's day parade. Usually held the Sunday after St. Patrick's day, it is the second largest parade in our area, after the New York City parade, and is great small town fun, featuring all of the area marching bands, bag pipers, fire engines and trucks. Montauk also hosts one of the many area Easter Egg hunts.

The official beginning of the summer high season, Memorial Day, is marked by the annual East Hampton Memorial Day parade, held on the Monday of Memorial Day weekend. The surrounding towns again bring out all of their fire trucks and antique cars but this parade is a bit more somber as the towns remember their fallen soldiers.

As Spring begins to flow into early summer, come out and pick your own strawberries at one of our many local farm stands. A stop at a farmers market on your way home yields an abundance of Spring's tender bounty- asparagus, strawberries, rhubarb and the first fresh herbs of the year.

Late May and early June bring two traditional East End pastimes. Whale watching off of Montauk begins in June and continues through the summer months. The Viking Fleet (516-668-5700) schedules regular excursions as well as providing ferry service to Block Island beginning in May.

The traditional start of the summer fishing season, the Blessing of the Fleet, takes place in Montauk Harbor and is said to bring luck to the fishermen as well as remembering those who died at sea during the previous year. The event itself is an exciting array of all types of boats from small private crafts to large commercial fishing boats that sail past the reviewing stands to receive the blessing of the local pastor for safety and success in the coming season.

Spring Menu I

Strawberry Rhubarb Compote

Brie and Herb Omelet Spirals

Lemon Glazed Tea Bread

Strawberry Rhubarb Compote

Yield: 6 servings

We love this as a way to take advantage of the all-too-brief rhubarb season. This dish is best served well-chilled. You can make this the night before, but don't add the strawberries until 30 to 60 minutes before you plan to serve it. We gratefully acknowledge Ken Haedrich's wonderful book **Country Breakfasts** *as the source for this dish.*

¾	pound fresh rhubarb (do not use frozen)
2	cups water
¾	cup sugar
1	teaspoon lemon zest
	Juice of ½ lemon
4	whole cloves
2	teaspoons minced candied ginger
1	pint fresh strawberries, hulled

✆ Put a shallow 13- by 9-inch baking dish or casserole, large enough to hold the rhubarb in one layer, in the freezer before you begin.

✆ Trim the rhubarb, discarding the leaves and any bruised or tough ends. Peel the rhubarb as you would celery, to remove the strings: get a sharp paring knife just under the surface and peel the stringy covering off the stalks. Put the peelings into a nonreactive saucepan with the water, sugar, lemon zest, lemon juice, and cloves. Bring to a boil, lower the heat slightly, then cover and boil gently for 5 minutes. Strain out the solids, reserving the liquid and return the liquid back into the original saucepan. Discard solids.

✆ Cut the peeled rhubarb into approximately ½-inch pieces. Cut any wide stalks in half lengthwise. Bring the reserved poaching liquid to a simmer and add the rhubarb. Simmer gently, partially covered, for 3 to 5 minutes; at the first sign of tenderness (pierce a piece with a paring knife), transfer the rhubarb from the liquid with a slotted spoon to the chilled casserole. Spread the rhubarb out in the casserole, then refrigerate, uncovered until cooled.

✆ While the rhubarb cools, bring the poaching liquid to a boil and reduce to about ½ cup. Pour it into a serving bowl and add the minced ginger. Cool to room temperature.

✆ If the strawberries are large, slice them into bite-size pieces; if they're small, just halve them. Add the strawberries and rhubarb to the poaching liquid. Toss gently, then refrigerate for 30 to 60 minutes before serving.

Brie and Herb Omelet Spirals

Yield: 8 servings

A beautiful way to serve eggs using fresh springtime herbs. The omelet is first rolled, jelly-roll style, then sliced to reveal the colorful interior.

9	eggs
3	tablespoons minced fresh parsley, chervil, and chives
	Salt and freshly ground pepper
3	tablespoons butter
4	ounces Brie cheese, rind removed, cut into ½-inch dice

❻ For each omelet: combine 3 eggs, 1 tablespoon of the herbs, and salt and pepper to taste in a small bowl. Beat lightly with a fork.

❻ Heat a heavy 6-inch omelet pan over medium-high heat. Add 1 tablespoon of the butter and heat until no longer foaming, tilting the pan to coat the bottom evenly. Add the egg mixture. Stir the eggs quickly, tilting the pan to keep the surface covered with egg and lifting the edges of the egg with the fork.

❻ When the eggs are almost set but still slightly creamy, sprinkle ⅓ of the diced Brie over the surface. Reduce the heat to low and cook until the Brie is melted and the surface of the omelet is firm. Roll the omelet up jelly-roll style and transfer it to a plate.

❻ Repeat with the remaining ingredients to make 2 more omelets.

❻ Chill the omelets in the refrigerator for 10 minutes to cool slightly. Cut crosswise into 1-inch-thick slices. Serve at room temperature.

Lemon Glazed Tea Bread

Yield: 2 loaves

Refreshing and delicious with breakfast, we also serve this bread as an afternoon snack with iced or hot tea. This bread can be prepared ahead. Wrap tightly in plastic wrap and refrigerate for 2 days or freeze up to 1 month. Serve at room temperature.

1	cup (2 sticks) butter, room temperature
2½	cups sugar
4	eggs, separated, room temperature
3¼	cups unbleached, all-purpose flour
4	teaspoons grated lemon peel
2	teaspoons baking powder
1	teaspoon salt
1¼	cups milk
¼	teaspoon cream of tartar
½	cup fresh lemon juice

⑥ Preheat the oven to 350°. Butter and line with parchment paper (2) 8½- by 4½-inch loaf pans.

⑥ In a large bowl of an electric mixer fitted with the paddle attachment, cream the butter with 2 cups of the sugar until light and fluffy. Beat in the yolks one at a time.

⑥ In a separate bowl, combine the flour, lemon peel, baking powder, and salt. Add to the butter mixture alternately with the milk, beginning and ending with the dry ingredients. Combine thoroughly after each addition.

⑥ In a separate bowl, beat the egg whites and the cream of tartar until stiff but not dry. Stir ⅓ of the egg whites into the butter-flour mixture to lighten the batter, then gently fold the remaining egg whites into the batter.

⑥ Divide the batter between the prepared pans. Bake 55 minutes or until a tester inserted in the center of each pan comes out clean. Cool the breads in the pans for 10 minutes. Invert onto racks to cool.

⑥ Mix the lemon juice and the remaining ½ cup of the sugar until the sugar dissolves. Pierce the surface of each loaf with a toothpick. Brush the hot loaves with lemon syrup, allowing the syrup to be absorbed. Cool completely.

Spring Menu II

Fresh Marinated Oranges with Cinnamon and Mint

Smoked Salmon and Vidalia Onion Tart with Grated Potato Crust

Sour Cream Loaf Cake

Irish Soda Bread

Fresh Marinated Oranges with Cinnamon and Mint

Yield: *4 servings*

Adapted from a recipe by Joan Morris at the Nuthatch Bed and Breakfast in Indianapolis, Indiana. A lively fruit dish to pep up the dull days before summer arrives, serve this dish in anticipation of the growing season.

4	seedless medium oranges
1	tablespoon lemon juice
¼	cup brown sugar
½	teaspoon cinnamon
⅛	teaspoon nutmeg
2	tablespoons fresh mint leaves

⑥ Peel the oranges removing all of the white pith. Cut the oranges crosswise into ¼-inch slices, retaining the round shape of the orange.

⑥ Place the oranges in a shallow 9- by 9-inch baking dish. Drizzle with the lemon juice.

⑥ In a small separate bowl, mix together the sugar, the cinnamon, and nutmeg. Sprinkle evenly over the oranges and between the slices. Cover tightly with plastic wrap and refrigerate for 8 hours or overnight. Occasionally baste the oranges with some of the lemon syrup.

⑥ At serving time, finely chop the fresh mint leaves. Spread each orange out onto overlapping slices and sprinkle with mint. Spoon some of the syrup over the oranges.

Smoked Salmon and Vidalia Onion Tart with Grated Potato Crust

Yield: 8 servings

This tart has an unusual grated potato crust. It's delicious with the creamy cheese and salty smoked salmon.

Crust:

2	cups packed, peeled and coarsely grated raw potato
1	teaspoon salt for absorbing, plus ½ teaspoon for seasoning
½	teaspoon pepper
1	egg, beaten
2	tablespoons light vegetable oil

Filling:

1	vidalia onion, finely chopped
1	teaspoon vegetable oil
6	eggs
½	cup whole milk (do not use fat free)
	Salt and pepper
2	teaspoons chopped fresh (or dried) dill
4	ounces cream cheese, cut into 1-inch cubes
4	ounces smoked salmon, cut into bite-sized pieces

To make the crust:

ⓑ Generously oil a 9-inch pie pan. Preheat the oven to 400°.

ⓑ Set the freshly grated potato in a colander over a bowl. Sprinkle 1 teaspoon salt over the top and leave it for 10 minutes, then squeeze out the excess water. Combine the grated potato, the remaining ½ teaspoon of the salt, the pepper, and egg in a medium bowl. Pat the potato mixture into the prepared pie pan, building up the sides of the crust with your fingers. Bake for 40 to 45 minutes until browned, brushing it after the first 30 minutes with the remaining oil to crispen the crust. Remove the tart crust from the oven and allow it to cool while preparing the filling.

To make the filling:

ⓑ Preheat the oven to 350°. Sauté the onion in 1 teaspoon of the vegetable oil until transparent but not brown. Remove from the heat and set aside.

ⓑ Combine the eggs and milk in a bowl and whisk until blended. Season with salt, pepper, and dill. Whisk to combine.

ⓑ Scatter the sautéed onion, cream cheese chunks and smoked salmon over the potato crust, spreading ingredients evenly. Pour the egg mixture over all, distributing evenly. Bake for 30 minutes or until the eggs are set.

Sour Cream Loaf Cake

Yield: 1 loaf

One of our favorite coffee cakes, it is delicately rich with a delightfully crunchy topping. Excellent with a cup of tea. Gratefully adapted from Chris Sprague's **Newcastle Inn Cookbook**.

2	cups unbleached all-purpose flour
1	teaspoon baking powder
1	teaspoon baking soda
½	teaspoon salt
½	cup (1 stick) unsalted butter, softened to room temperature
2	eggs
1½	cups sugar
1	cup sour cream
1	teaspoon vanilla extract
½	cup coarsely chopped walnuts
1	teaspoon ground cinnamon

⚑ Preheat the oven to 350°. Grease well and flour an 8- by 4-inch loaf pan.

⚑ In a mixing bowl, sift together the flour, baking powder, baking soda, and salt.

⚑ In the bowl of an electric mixer fitted with the paddle attachment, cream the butter with 1 cup of the sugar until light and fluffy, approximately 5 minutes. Add the eggs and beat until blended.

⚑ Add the flour mixture to the creamed mixture in thirds, alternating with the sour cream and ending with the flour mixture. Add the vanilla, and mix just until blended.

⚑ Combine the remaining ½ cup of the sugar with the walnuts and the cinnamon in a small bowl.

⚑ Pour half the batter into the prepared loaf pan. Sprinkle half the nut mixture over the batter. Top with remaining batter and sprinkle with the nut mixture.

⚑ Bake for about 45 minutes or until a toothpick inserted into the center comes clean. Cool in the pan for 10 minutes before removing the cake.

Irish Soda Bread

Yield: 1 loaf

When we have traveled in Ireland, we've noticed that Irish Soda bread is generally not very sweet, often with neither raisins nor caraway seeds. This bread is more typical of an Irish scone. It is sweet and rich and absolutely delicious in its own right.

3½	cups unbleached all-purpose flour
⅔	cup sugar
1	teaspoon salt
1	tablespoon baking powder
1	teaspoon baking soda
1½	cups raisins
1	tablespoon caraway seeds
2	eggs
1½	cups buttermilk
2	tablespoons melted butter

⑥ Preheat the oven to 375°. Grease a 9-by 5-inch loaf pan.

⑥ Sift together the flour, sugar, salt, baking powder and baking soda into a large mixing bowl. Stir in the raisins and caraway seeds. Coat the raisins with the dry ingredients.

⑥ In a separate bowl, whisk together the eggs, buttermilk and the melted butter.

⑥ Add the liquid ingredients to the dry ingredients; mix until blended.

⑥ Pour the batter into the prepared loaf pan. Bake in the oven for one hour or until a toothpick inserted in the center comes clean.

Summer

Sagaponack Lake, a view from the bridge

Sagaponack (Summer)

These reeds I see are full of tears:

summer rain simplified by grass,

the pathway of water interrupted by matter.

As it falls the blue heron steps

through grains of a great web.

Sand, reeds, rain

translucent as years,

water tangible as tears

on grasses by the salt pond.

Called globes, each orb of rain

touched by grass, fluid in rest,

reflects reeds, wings, the surface glitter of summer,

clarity of dwelling in one body.

–Scott Chaskey

Summer Pleasures

The high summer season in the Hamptons is so chock full of activities and events for the visitor to enjoy that one could easily overlook the great natural beauty of our area. So we urge you, don't miss the beaches. They are some of the world's finest and we encourage you to take time out to enjoy a long walk down East Hampton's Main Beach or a spectacular sunset at Sag Harbor's Long Beach, perhaps with a picnic supper. Then move on to the whirl wind of fun that awaits you.

Throughout East Hampton, Sag Harbor and Southampton various organizations put on good old fashioned summer carnivals featuring rides and games, food and fireworks- it's a paradise for kids of all ages. Don't miss the Southampton Kiwanis carnival in June and the East Hampton Ladies Village Improvement Society fair in July.

The Hamptons in summer were made for outdoor activities. Main Beach Surf and Sport shop in Wainscott (516-537-2716) can supply all the gear you need for kayaking, canoeing or in-line skating. Fishing continues throughout the summer months. Check out the Lazy Bones (516-668-5700) or Sport Fishing Charter Service (516-668-2707) in Montauk for fishing excursions, but you can also just cast off the beach or the town dock on Gann Road in Springs.

Other activities to partake in include horseback riding at Deep Hollow Ranch in Montauk, the oldest continually operating ranch in the United States (516- 668-2744). We also love to bicycle around; it's a great alternative to the car during this peak traffic season. For bike rentals try Bermuda Bikes in East Hampton (516-324-6688) or Cycle Path in Amagansett (516-267-6313).

Then, of course, there are the events. In July there are fabulous Fourth of July fireworks displays in East Hampton as well as all of the surrounding villages. Then there is the Music Festival of the Hamptons in late July; with ongoing performances in several venues of both world renowned and up and coming musicians.

The Artists and Writers Softball game, an annual charitable event, brings together such local celebrities as Paul Simon, Alec Baldwin and Dick Cavett in a semi-serious competition at the East Hampton Village softball field in mid-July.

The crowning event of the season is the Hampton Classic Horse Show. Held the last week of August in Bridgehampton, it brings together world class and novice equestrian talent from around the country for a week of competition culminating in the Grand Prix on the last day. Even if you're not a rider, there is plenty of shopping at the kiosks and a Saturday kid's day with a petting zoo, clowns and pony rides.

Finally on Labor Day Weekend, experience another aspect of the Hamptons at the annual Shinnecock Tribes' Pow-Wow. The Shinnecock Tribe along with the Montauketts were among the original settlers of the Hamptons and they honor their heritage with three days of traditional Native American dancing, competitions and foods held on the Shinnecock Reservation in Southampton.

Summer Menu I

Mixed Melon Salad with Fresh Mint

Baked Blueberry Blintzes with Vanilla Custard

Orange Sour Cream Loaf

Mixed Melon Salad with Fresh Mint
Yield: 6 servings

Although this is a very simple fruit dish the secret is to use the freshest possible ingredients and take advantage of what is in season. Choose a selection of ripe summer melons. Our favorites are Crenshaws, Cantaloupes, Honeydews, and our own local Musk Melons.

3	ripe melons of choice
¼	cup fresh mint leaves

ᕬ Cut each melon in half and scoop out the seeds. Using a melon baller scoop out balls from each melon and place them into a large serving bowl.

ᕬ Coarsely chop the mint leaves and sprinkle over the melons, mixing gently with a rubber spatula to combine. Chill before serving.

Orange Sour Cream Loaf
Yield: 1 loaf

A rich fruit-flavored bread, this is one of our most requested breakfast breads.

½	cup (1 stick) butter, softened
1	cup sugar
2	eggs
1	tablespoon orange zest
2	cups unbleached, all-purpose flour
1	teaspoon baking powder
½	teaspoon baking soda
½	teaspoon salt
1	cup sour cream (low fat is fine to use)

ᕬ Grease a 9- by 5-inch loaf pan. Preheat the oven to 350°.

ᕬ In the bowl of an electric mixer fitted with the paddle attachment, beat the butter and sugar until fluffy. Add the eggs and orange zest. Combine thoroughly.

ᕬ In a separate medium-sized bowl, combine the flour, baking powder, baking soda, and salt.

ᕬ Add the dry ingredients to the butter mixture, alternating with the sour cream in 3 additions beginning and ending with the dry ingredients. Blend completely after each addition. Pour the batter into the prepared pan and bake in the oven for 1 hour or until a toothpick inserted in the center comes clean.

Baked Blueberry Blintzes with Vanilla Custard

Yield: 24 crêpes

We serve this as a casserole buffet breakfast dish. Our guests also love the blintzes simply sautéed in butter until browned and sprinkled with powdered sugar.

Crêpes:

1	cup water
1	cup low-fat milk
4	eggs
½	teaspoon salt
2	cups all-purpose flour
4	tablespoons butter, melted

Filling:

2	cups (2 percent) cottage cheese
1	cup low-fat sour cream
½	cup sugar
1	tablespoon vanilla extract
2	teaspoons cinnamon
1	pint fresh blueberries; washed and stems removed, reserving 2 tablespoons for garnish

Custard:

2	eggs
3	tablespoons sugar
1	teaspoon vanilla extract
1	cup low-fat milk

To make crêpes:

⑥ Mix all of the crêpe ingredients in a blender until smooth. Refrigerate for 2 hours or overnight.

⑥ Coat a non-stick 8-inch crêpe or omelette pan with cooking oil spray. For each crêpe, spoon in 1 ounce of batter and swirl to cover the bottom of pan. Cook for 30 seconds. Loosen the edge of the crêpe and turn. Cook for 10 seconds longer. Remove from the pan; repeat with the remaining batter. Cool the crêpes and stack them between layers of wax paper. Do not overlap the crêpes as they may stick together.

To make filling:

⑥ Combine the cottage cheese, sour cream, sugar, vanilla, and cinnamon in a medium sized mixing bowl. Using a rubber spatula, gently fold in the blueberries.

(*Baked Blueberry Blintzes continued*)

To form blintzes:

ⓑ Coat a 9- by 9-inch baking pan with cooking oil spray. For each blintz, lay 1 crêpe on a flat surface. Spoon 1 tablespoon of the filling onto the center of crêpe. Fold the bottom end over the filling, fold in the center edges and roll up. Place the blintz seam-side down in the prepared baking pan. Repeat with the remaining crêpes and filling, lining up the finished blintzes in the baking pan.

To make custard:

ⓑ Preheat the oven to 400°. Combine all of the custard ingredients together in a medium mixing bowl. Beat together with a whisk until well blended.

ⓑ Pour the custard evenly over the blintzes and bake in the oven for 30 to 35 minutes or until golden brown. Sprinkle with the reserved 2 tablespoons of blueberries and serve immediately.

Summer Menu II

Mixed Fresh Berries with Crème Anglaise

Smoked-Salmon and Cream-Cheese Quesadillas

Coconut Banana Bread

Mixed Fresh Berries with Crème Anglaise   Yield: 8 servings

Another simple summer fruit dish, we especially love this dish when we can use our own local strawberries. We use the freshest, most beautiful berries we can find. Crème anglaise, or english custard is a smooth and silky, vanilla flavored sauce, delicious with fresh fruits, pastries or bread pudding. We use cookbook author Marion Cunningham's crème anglaise recipe, we think it's the best. Add this to your sauce repertoire.

6	cups mixed berries (such as strawberries, blueberries, raspberries, blackberries)
2	cups milk
½	cup sugar
4	egg yolks
⅛	teaspoon salt
2	teaspoons pure vanilla extract
8	sprigs fresh mint leaves for garnish

Ⓑ Rinse the berries under cool water and gently mix in a large bowl using a rubber spatula; set aside.

Ⓑ Heat the milk in a heavy bottomed saucepan to simmering (small bubbles will form around the edges of the pan); remove from heat. Add the sugar and whisk to dissolve.

Ⓑ In a separate bowl, lightly beat the egg yolks. Pour ¼ cup of the hot milk over the egg yolks, stirring briskly.

Ⓑ Add the yolk mixture back to the rest of the milk; return to the stove over low heat and add the salt. Cook stirring constantly for several minutes until you begin to see the sauce thicken.

Ⓑ Remove from the heat and pour through a fine sieve or strainer into a bowl. Add the vanilla, stirring briefly to help the sauce cool. Refrigerate to cool completely. The sauce will thicken somewhat as it cools.

Ⓑ Divide the berries between 8 fruit bowls or wine goblets. Drizzle about ¼ cup of crème anglaise over each serving and garnish with a fresh mint sprig.

Smoked-Salmon and Cream-Cheese Quesadillas

Yield: *12 servings*

This is one of our most popular summer breakfast dishes. Some of our returning guests now request this breakfast when they make their reservations. We usually make extra so that we can enjoy it for a cool summer lunch.

6	ounces low-fat cream cheese; softened to room temperature
2	tablespoons chopped fresh dill, plus 2 teaspoons for garnish
1	tablespoon fresh lemon juice
6	8-inch flour tortillas (white or whole-wheat)
12	ounces smoked salmon
	Salt and pepper
3	scallions chopped, green parts only
1	lemon, thinly sliced into rounds

🌀 In the bowl of an electric mixer combine the cream cheese, 2 tablespoons of the dill, salt and pepper to taste, and lemon juice. Beat until smooth and well blended. Set aside.

🌀 In a 10-inch non-stick skillet, warm each tortilla over low heat until lightly browned on each side. Set aside on a cookie sheet.

🌀 For each quesadilla: Spread about 2 tablespoons of the cream cheese mixture evenly on a tortilla, covering to the edges. Arrange 2 ounces of the sliced smoked salmon over the cheese, covering to the edges. Repeat with the remaining tortillas. Sprinkle with the reserved 2 teaspoons of chopped dill. Cut each tortilla into 6 wedges. Use 4 wedges per serving. Garnish with lemon slices and sprinkle with scallions.

Coconut Banana Bread

Yield: 1 loaf

The addition of the coconut gives this banana bread a slight crunch and an extra special flavor. Our youngest visitors to the Mill House especially love this banana bread. We hope you will, too.

1	cup flaked sweetened coconut
¼	cup (½ stick) butter
⅔	cup sugar
2	eggs
3	tablespoons milk
1	teaspoon lemon juice
½	teaspoon almond extract
2	cups unbleached, all-purpose flour
1	teaspoon baking powder
½	teaspoon baking soda
½	teaspoon salt
1	cup mashed banana (2 bananas)

◐ Preheat the oven to 350°. Grease a 9- by 5-inch loaf pan.

◐ Spread the coconut on a cookie sheet, breaking up any lumps with your fingers. Bake for 15 minutes, stirring once during the baking time to promote even browning. Remove from the oven and set aside, but don't turn off the oven.

◐ In the bowl of an electric mixer fitted with the paddle attachment, cream together the butter and sugar. Beat in the eggs. Stir in the milk, lemon juice and almond extract.

◐ In a separate bowl, mix together the flour, baking powder, baking soda and salt; add to the butter mixture. Mix in the bananas; fold in the coconut.

◐ Pour the batter into the prepared pan and bake for 1 hour or until a toothpick inserted in the center comes clean.

Summer Menu III

Tomato-Basil-Onion Frittata

Fruit and Yogurt Pizza

Buttermilk Corn Bread

Tomato-Basil-Onion Frittata

Yield: 2 servings

We wait anxiously until the first tomatoes from our garden ripen and we have fresh basil before we make this frittata. It is well worth the wait. Our guests love this for breakfast, but it is also a wonderful lunch or light summer supper dish.

2	tablespoons olive oil
2	medium ripe tomatoes, cut in medium dice
½	medium onion, finely chopped
	Salt and pepper
½	cup fresh basil leaves, chopped
6	eggs
4	tablespoons milk

In a medium skillet, heat the oil and sauté the tomatoes and onion. Add salt and pepper to taste. Turn off the heat and mix in the basil (if there is a lot of liquid in the pan, drain off before making frittata).

Lightly coat an 8-inch non-stick omelette pan with cooking oil spray. Add ½ of the tomato-basil mixture and cook it over medium heat.

In a small bowl, whisk together 3 of the eggs with 2 tablespoons of the milk.

Pour the egg mixture into the omelette pan, distributing evenly over the tomato-basil mixture; stir gently with a rubber spatula to combine. Allow the eggs to cook for a minute or 2 to set the bottom. Then using a rubber spatula gently lift an edge of the eggs and tipping the pan, allow uncooked egg mixture to run underneath building up the height of the frittata. Continue this gentle cooking process until the eggs are nearly cooked through, about 5 minutes. To finish cooking the top of the frittata, slide the pan into a preheated broiler for a minute or 2. Repeat this procedure for the second frittata.

Fruit and Yogurt Pizza

Yield: 8 to 10 servings

A beautiful and festive dish, we often serve this on hot summer mornings. You may want to make the yogurt topping an hour ahead of serving time or the night before.

Toppings:

2   (8-ounce) containers vanilla or lemon yogurt
3   cups thinly sliced assorted fruit (such as blueberries, strawberries, peaches, cantaloupe, blackberries, raspberries)

Crust:

1⅓   cups unbleached, all-purpose flour
1½   tablespoons sugar
2   teaspoons grated lemon peel
10   tablespoons well-chilled unsalted butter, cut into bits
3   tablespoons water, or more if needed to make dough pliable

To make the yogurt topping:

⑤ Drain the yogurt in a strainer lined with either a double layer of cheesecloth or a large coffee filter set over a bowl in the refrigerator for at least 1 hour or overnight. (Most of the moisture will have drained out making the yogurt of spreading consistency.) Reserve the yogurt in the refrigerator while preparing the crust.

To make the pizza crust:

⑤ Combine the flour, sugar, and lemon peel in the bowl of an electric mixer fitted with the paddle attachment. Blend in the butter until the mixture resembles coarse meal. Mix in enough water to bind the dough.

⑤ Gather the dough into a ball and flatten into a disc. Wrap the dough in plastic wrap and refrigerate for 30 minutes.

⑤ Roll the dough out onto a lightly floured surface to a 12-inch round. Transfer to a baking sheet or pizza pan. Crimp the edges to form the rim. Pierce all over with a fork. Freeze for 30 minutes. Preheat the oven to 375°. Bake until the crust is golden brown, about 25 to 30 minutes. Cool completely before proceeding.

Assembly:

⑤ Spread the reserved yogurt evenly over the cooled pizza crust.

⑤ Arrange the fruits decoratively on top of the yogurt, filling the entire crust generously with an assortment of fruits.

(*Fruit and Yogurt Pizza continued*)

Alternative Pizza Topping Using Cream Cheese:

2   (8-ounce) bars cream cheese, room temperature
½   cup strawberry preserves

In the bowl of an electric mixer fitted with the paddle attachment, cream together the cream cheese and preserves. Spread evenly over the cooled pizza crust covering to the edge of the crust. Layer the fruit over the cream cheese as previously described.

Buttermilk Corn Bread

Yield: 1 loaf

During the summer months, we sometimes offer our guests a southern-style breakfast with grits, biscuits, eggs, ham and this deliciously moist corn bread. We also enjoy it ourselves as a quick breakfast or a nutritious snack.

1	cup stone-ground cornmeal
1	cup unbleached, all-purpose flour
1	teaspoon baking powder
1	teaspoon baking soda
¾	teaspoon salt
½	cup sugar
1¼	cups buttermilk
2	eggs
4	tablespoons melted butter

⑥ Preheat the oven to 400°. Grease and flour an 8- by 4-inch loaf pan.

⑥ In a mixing bowl, stir together the cornmeal, flour, baking powder, baking soda, salt and sugar.

⑥ In a separate bowl whisk together the buttermilk, eggs and the melted butter.

⑥ Add the liquid ingredients to the cornmeal mixture, stirring just to combine (do not overmix).

⑥ Pour the batter into the prepared pan and bake for 30 to 35 minutes or until a toothpick inserted in the center comes clean.

Autumn

Quail Hill Organic Farm in Amagansett

Autumn Equinox

September rain falls on oaks,

darkens the tidal reeds.

Over first frost

and fall of the leaf

no longer a child

in summer's sky

moon lights her last crickets

in grasses and grains.

Sparrows, swallows circle and flock

when night equals day at equinox.

Soon Harvest Moon

will light autumn fruits

that fall, like small suns or last leaves

through a tender clasp of space.

–*Scott Chaskey*

Autumn, Our Glorious Indian Summer

When you live in the Hamptons year round, you live for the Autumn. In September and October the number of visitors thins out a bit and the weather is glorious. Warm days and cooler evenings bring the gradual turning of the leaves to reveal their brilliant hues. We drive past the farm stands and marvel at the symphony of colors - orange, burgundy and gold as the Fall harvest spills out of the bins.

It is a delightful time to be outdoors. We encourage you to explore the East End by hiking our many nature trails (contact the Southampton Trails Preservation Society at 516-537-5207 for information), take a leisurely ride on a bicycle or go apple or pumpkin picking at one of the farm stands.

For golf fans, there is still plenty of great weather to enjoy a round or two at one of our many excellent and varied courses. There is a championship course at Montauk Downs State Park and Poxabogue is a good par-3 course in Bridgehampton with many other options in between.

This is the time of year to visit the Long Island Wineries. A day trip from the city or part of a weekend getaway, the North Fork of Long Island is home to 17 small winemakers with three others located on the South Fork. Starting out from East Hampton, we usually take the ferries across Shelter Island, which in itself is a beautiful ride, and then drive West through the villages of the North Fork, stopping along the way to enjoy tours and tastings at the various wineries. With its rural agrarian vistas, the North Fork of Long Island has reinvented itself from producing primarily the famed Long Island potatoes and ducks to a viable industry of winemakers who are beginning to produce world class wines.

Other Autumn pursuits include browsing the abundant antique shops located throughout the Hamptons (some of the most interesting, in our opinion, are in Sag Harbor) or taking in a film at the Hamptons International Film Festival which is held in East Hampton usually the third week of October (Call the film festival office at 516-324-4600 for information). This film festival features independent and novice film makers and it's always possible that you may be watching a future hit.

The Hallockville Farm Museum, located in Riverhead (516-298-5292), hosts several fall and early winter festivals which are wonderful old fashioned fun and are a great day out with kids. In particular, come on out for the Annual Fall Festival, held in October, featuring arts and crafts vendors, music, crafts demonstrations, hayrides, and food. Early American holiday preparations are the focus of "Thanksgiving on the Farm", in November as is the "Victorian Christmas Open House" held in early December.

Autumn Menu I

Broiled Grapefruit with Cinnamon Sugar

Pumpkin-Cornmeal Pancakes

Broiled Grapefruit
with Cinnamon Sugar

Yield: 2 servings

Our guests love this simple cold weather fruit dish. They are always surprised to discover how sweet and delicious warm grapefruit can be.

1   large pink or white grapefruit
1   teaspoon ground cinnamon
2   tablespoons granulated brown sugar
1   strawberry, halved or 1 kiwi, skin removed and cut into ¼-inch round slices

⑥ Preheat the oven to 400°.

⑥ Cut the grapefruit in half crosswise. Cut around each section to loosen with a grapefruit or serrated knife. Place each half on an ovenproof cookie sheet.

⑥ Sprinkle each half with 1 tablespoon of the brown sugar and ¼ teaspoon of the cinnamon.

⑥ Bake for 10 minutes, then run under the broiler for 3 to 4 minutes, until the edges of the grapefruit are slightly browned. Serve warm, garnished with the strawberry or kiwi slice in the center of each grapefruit half.

Pumpkin-Cornmeal Pancakes

Yield: 12 pancakes

These pancakes are as light as a feather. They are especially delicious with pure maple syrup on a chilly morning.

¾	cup unbleached all-purpose flour
¾	cup cornmeal (preferably stone-ground)
¼	cup firmly packed brown sugar
1½	teaspoons baking powder
1	teaspoon pumpkin pie spice (or substitute ½ teaspoon cinnamon and ½ teaspoon allspice)
½	teaspoon baking soda
1	teaspoon salt
1⅔	cups low-fat buttermilk
¾	cup pumpkin puree
2	tablespoons vegetable oil
2	whole eggs
1	egg white

⑥ Combine the flour, cornmeal, brown sugar, baking powder, spice, baking soda, and salt in a large bowl; stir well.

⑥ In a separate medium bowl, combine the buttermilk, pumpkin, oil, egg whites, and egg yolks. Whisk together until well combined. Add to the flour mixture, stirring until smooth.

⑥ Spoon about ⅓ cup batter for each pancake onto a hot nonstick griddle or nonstick skillet (if necessary, griddle can be coated with cooking oil spray). Cook 2 minutes on first side or until golden brown (bubbles will not form on tops of pancakes, and edges will not look cooked). Turn pancake over and cook 2 more minutes on second side.

Autumn Menu II

Potato and Cheese Frittata with Southwestern Chili Sauce

Apple Cranberry Crisp

Oatmeal Bread

Cranberry-Orange Pecan Scones

Potato and Cheese Frittata with Southwestern Chili Sauce

Yield: 2 frittatas

We love the combination of potatoes and cheese in a frittata. We created the sauce as an interesting alternative to plain ketchup, which many of our guests like with their eggs. There will be extra sauce for use in another recipe.

Sauce:

1	tablespoon olive oil
½	medium onion finely chopped
1	28-ounce can crushed tomatoes
1	cup water
1	teaspoon sugar
1½	teaspoons ground coriander
1½	teaspoons ground cumin
1½	teaspoons chili powder
	Salt and black pepper
½	cup canned, chopped mild green chili peppers

Frittata:

1	baking potato
1	tablespoon olive oil
2	tablespoons finely chopped scallions
	Salt and pepper
6	eggs
6	tablespoons milk
6	ounces Monterey Jack cheese

To make the sauce:

⑥ In a medium saucepan, heat the olive oil and add the onion. Sauté over medium heat until softened, but not browned.

⑥ Add the crushed tomatoes, water, sugar, coriander, cumin, chili powder and chili peppers. Season with salt and pepper. Stir to combine. Bring to a boil, then simmer for 20 to 30 minutes until the sauce is thickened. Remove from the heat and reserve. (The sauce can be made ahead of time and reheated at serving time, thinned with water if necessary.)

Frittata:

⑥ Peel the potato, then cut it in half vertically and thinly slice each half horizontally to form half-moon slices. Sauté the potato in olive oil until cooked through and golden brown. Season with salt and pepper to taste. Add scallions and stir to combine. Remove from the heat.

(*Potato and Cheese Frittata continued*)

ⓑ For each frittata: Lightly coat a nonstick, 8-inch omelet pan with cooking oil spray. Add ½ of the potato-scallion mixture and cook over medium heat.

ⓑ In a small bowl, whisk together 3 eggs with 2 tablespoons of milk and 3 tablespoons of the cheese.

ⓑ Pour the egg mixture into the omelet pan, distributing evenly over the potato mixture. Stir gently to combine the ingredients and allow the eggs to cook for a minute or so to set the bottom. Then using a rubber spatula gently lift an edge of the eggs and tipping the pan, allow uncooked egg mixture to run underneath the eggs, building up the height of the frittata. Continue this gentle cooking process until the eggs are nearly cooked through, about 5 minutes. To finish cooking the top of the frittata, slide the pan into a preheated broiler for a minute or so. Repeat this procedure for the second frittata.

ⓑ Slide the finished frittata out of the pan and onto a plate.

ⓑ Reheat the tomato and chili sauce and serve on the side.

Apple Cranberry Crisp

Yield: 6 to 8 servings

Although we serve this dish to our guests as a winter breakfast fruit, we also enjoy it as a dessert topped with vanilla ice cream.

The topping is wonderful to sprinkle on any baked fruit dish or on top of a streusel coffee cake before baking. We usually make a large batch of the topping and store it in the freezer. We purchase our very popular low fat Mainely Maple Granola Cereal by mail order from GrandyOats located in Maine (207) 647-4100.

Topping:

½   cup brown sugar
½   cup all-purpose flour
¾   stick chilled butter cut into ¼-inch bits
½   cup old-fashioned rolled oats
½   cup quality granola (preferably fat free)

Filling:

8   tart apples, such as Granny Smith; peeled and cored and cut into a medium dice
2   tablespoons fresh lemon juice (from about ½ medium lemon)
1   cup whole fresh cranberries
1   teaspoon cinnamon
¼   cup brown sugar
¼   cup orange juice
1   teaspoon cornstarch

⑥ Preheat the oven to 375°. Lightly butter a shallow 9- by 9-inch baking dish.

⑥ In the bowl of a food processor fitted with the metal blade, combine the sugar, flour, butter, and oats. Pulse until the mixture resembles coarse meal. Transfer the mixture to a mixing bowl and stir in the granola. Set aside.

⑥ In a medium bowl, combine the apples with the lemon juice. Add the cranberries, cinnamon, brown sugar, orange juice and cornstarch; stir to blend.

⑥ Pour the apple mixture into the prepared baking dish and sprinkle generously with the topping. Bake for 45 minutes or until the fruit mixture is bubbling and the topping is golden brown.

Oatmeal Bread

Yield: *2 loaves*

Although this is a quick bread, it has an almost yeast bread texture. Not too sweet, it is excellent for toasting. We usually serve it for breakfast but it is also lovely with tea.

2	cups milk
2	cups plus 2 tablespoons old-fashioned oats
4	eggs
1½	sticks butter, melted
½	cup brown sugar
4	cups unbleached, all purpose flour
4½	teaspoons baking powder
1	teaspoon salt

⑥ Preheat the oven to 350°. Grease (2) 8-by 4-inch loaf pans.

⑥ In a mixing bowl, combine the milk and 2 cups of oats; let stand for 5 minutes.

⑥ Mix in the eggs, butter and sugar and blend well. Stir in the flour, baking powder, and salt.

⑥ Pour the batter into the prepared pans. Sprinkle with the reserved 2 tablespoons of oats. Bake in the oven for 50 to 55 minutes or until a toothpick inserted in the center comes clean.

Cranberry-Orange Pecan Scones

Yield: 10 scones

Adapted from a recipe from **Country Breakfasts** *by Ken Haedrich, these scones are a divine combination of rich, tart, and sweet. You can also substitute fresh or dried blueberries or raisins for the cranberries. Do not use frozen blueberries, they contain too much liquid and make the dough too wet.*

2	cups unbleached, all-purpose flour
⅓	cup sugar
3	tablespoons wheat germ
1	teaspoon baking soda
1	teaspoon baking powder
½	teaspoon salt
6	tablespoons cold, unsalted butter cut into ¼-inch pieces
1	cup sour cream
1	large egg
1	teaspoon lemon extract
½	teaspoon vanilla extract
	Finely grated zest of 1 orange
1½	cups fresh or dried cranberries
½	cup chopped fresh pecans
¼	cup milk

⌥ Preheat the oven to 400°. Lightly coat 2 large cookie sheets with cooking oil spray.

⌥ In a large bowl, mix the flour, sugar, wheat germ, baking soda, baking powder, and salt. Add the butter and cut it in, using your fingers or a pastry blender, until the mixture resembles corn meal.

⌥ In a separate bowl, whisk together the sour cream, egg, extracts, and orange zest. Make a well in the center of the dry ingredients; add the liquid and quickly mix to blend. Gently fold in the cranberries and the pecans.

⌥ The dough will be sticky, so form the scones using floured hands. Use a spoon to scoop enough dough into floured hands to form a scone. Round it gently and place the scone on the prepared cookie sheet. Repeat for the remaining scones, leaving some room between for spreading. Using a pastry brush, gently brush each scone with some milk.

⌥ Bake for 20 minutes until golden brown. Cool for several minutes before serving.

Winter

Wainscott Pond at Wainscott Main Street

Winter Solstice

As high as two

bright stars

by the Hare's feet

Sun completes

the journey south.

Corn, beans, squash seeds

sleep in the earth with stone.

time to plant prayer sticks

in winter ground and wait.

Light the new fire!

By these words,

Come North, Sun!

From the Hare's feet,

warm water and air

and the chambers

of the earth, for seeds.

—*Scott Chaskey*

Winter Holiday Fun

As we move into the winter holiday season, we eagerly anticipate the appearance of the first Christmas wreaths and twinkling lights which pierce the darkness of the early winter nights. Before the lull of January and February, the month of December is filled with festive events.

The first Saturday of December brings the annual Santa parade down Main Street in East Hampton. In addition to the ubiquitous fire engines and trucks, this parade attracts many colorful floats created by local organizations and businesses and the finale is always the first appearance of Santa riding in the last fire engine. The day continues with a free childrens' film at the East Hampton movie theater.

The holiday tree lighting ceremony at the Maidstone Arms Inn and Restaurant in East Hampton, occurs on an early December Friday evening and is a festive evening of caroling with hot chocolate and cookies offered to the children. This is also the beginning of the annual "Toys for Tots" gift giving program in our community.

One of our favorite holiday activities is the Tour of Historic Inns and Houses in East Hampton (Call the East Hampton Chamber of Commerce at 516-324-0362 for information). This is a fun filled Saturday of visiting some of the many interesting homes and charming historical buildings in East Hampton. At each stop on the tour, visitors can marvel at the beautiful home and creativity in holiday decorations as well as enjoying a grazing lunch with different houses providing hors d'oeuvres, beverages and desserts.

Another local holiday tradition is the Choral Society of the Hamptons annual holiday concert, held on a Sunday afternoon and evening in December at the Bridgehampton Presbyterian Church. In addition to a beautiful rendering of familiar carols, the program will include an ambitious longer piece, often unusual, but always interesting. Throughout the villages of the East End there are an abundance of tree lighting ceremonies, concerts and house tours making this season especially festive.

After the celebrations of New Year's Eve, the East End quiets down for a few weeks in January and February. This is an excellent time of year to journey out for a quiet getaway weekend. Enjoy a spa day at Gurney's Resort in Montauk (516-668-2345) and then take advantage of the prix fixe specials at many of the area's best restaurants. Top it off with a stay at the Mill House Inn and enjoy our cozy rooms, gas fireplaces and whirlpool baths. East Hampton also has a winter tradition of wonderful semi-professional community theater with several shows each winter staged at Guild Hall (516-324-0806).

Because the ocean breezes keep our area somewhat warmer than other parts of the mid-atlantic in winter, we don't often get an abundance of snowfall. When it snows though, people love to get out their cross country skis and head out to the golf courses or parks and the air is filled with the joyful sounds of children sledding down a hill. Once in a while the town pond will freeze over and you'll see the children out ice skating and playing hockey.

Winter Menu I

Orange and Kiwi Swirl with Toasted Coconut

Pumpkin-Apple Bread Pudding

with Cranberry Maple Compote

Orange and Kiwi Swirl with Toasted Coconut

Yield: 4 servings

The color and arrangement of this dish works well on a buffet by arranging alternating rounds of orange and kiwi on a decorative serving platter and sprinkling generously with the toasted coconut.

The secret to peeling the oranges as described in this recipe is to make sure that your knife is very sharp. This technique also works well with grapefruit.

½	cup shredded sweetened coconut
4	oranges (preferably seedless)
2	kiwis

⑥ Preheat the oven to 350°. Spread the coconut on a cookie sheet, breaking up any lumps with your fingers. Bake in the oven for 15 minutes or until golden brown. Stir the coconut once or twice during the cooking time to promote even browning. Check the oven often as coconut burns easily. Remove from the oven and reserve.

⑥ Remove the skin from the oranges by first slicing a circle off of each end. Then put the orange on a cutting board, standing it up on a cut end. Using a very sharp paring or small utility knife, remove the orange skin and white pith by cutting down the length of the orange from top to bottom, following the curve of the orange and taking as little of the orange itself as possible. Rotate the orange until all of the skin and white pith is removed. The result should be a perfectly clean and round orange. Repeat with remaining oranges. Slice each orange into 4 round slices.

⑥ Remove the skin from the kiwi fruit and slice each kiwi into 8 round slices.

⑥ For each serving: layer 4 orange rounds alternately with 4 kiwi rounds across a plate. Sprinkle each serving with 1 tablespoon of the reserved toasted coconut.

Pumpkin-Apple Bread Pudding with Cranberry Maple Compote

Yield: 6 servings

A lighter variation of the typical bread pudding using our favorite fall ingredients, this pudding is a Mill House favorite. The slight tang of the cranberry compote perfectly complements the sweet spiciness of the pudding. We use different breads, homemade type white is good, so are french baguettes or a homemade type whole grain bread. Feel free to experiment.

Cranberry maple compote:

12	ounces fresh whole cranberries
1	cup orange juice
1	cup water
½	cup pure maple syrup
¼	cup granulated brown sugar

Bread Pudding:

5	cups dry bread cut into 1-inch cubes
1	teaspoon ground cinnamon
1	teaspoon pumpkin pie spice
3	tablespoons unsalted butter, melted
3	whole eggs
2	eggs-separated
1	cup milk
1	cup canned pumpkin puree
½	cup pure maple syrup
1	teaspoon vanilla extract
3	tart apples (such as Granny Smith, Mackintosh or Macoun) peeled, cored and chopped into 1-inch pieces

To make the cranberry compote:

⑥ Combine all of the ingredients in a medium saucepan. Bring to a boil over medium heat. Reduce the heat to low and simmer for 25 minutes stirring occasionally until a medium-thick sauce consistency is achieved. Mash some of the cranberries against the sides of the pan with a spoon to help them dissolve. The sauce can be thinned with water if necessary and reheated before serving.

To make the bread pudding:

⑥ Preheat the oven to 350°. In a large bowl toss the bread cubes with the cinnamon, pumpkin pie spice, and melted butter.

⑥ In a separate bowl, whisk together the 3 whole eggs and the 2 egg yolks. Add the milk, pumpkin, maple syrup and vanilla. Pour the milk mixture over the bread cubes. Blend thoroughly and refrigerate for 1 hour or overnight.

(*Pumpkin-Apple* Bread Pudding *continued*)

◐ Before baking, lightly butter a 9- by 9-inch shallow baking dish. Whisk together the 2 reserved egg whites until they hold soft peaks.

◐ Stir the apples into the bread mixture. Stir about ⅓ of the beaten egg whites into the bread mixture to lighten it. Then gently fold in the remaining whipped egg whites. Pour the mixture into the prepared baking dish.

◐ Place the casserole with the bread mixture into a baking pan large enough to hold it. Fill the larger pan about 1-inch with boiling water. Place in the oven and bake for 50 minutes or until the pudding is set. Remove the pudding from the water bath and let cool for about 10 minutes before serving. Serve with the cranberry maple compote.

Winter Menu II

Baked Fruit Casserole

Individual Baked Eggs Florentine

Pumpkin Raisin Cake

Whole Grain Irish Soda Bread

Baked Fruit Casserole

Yield: *10 servings*

Adapted from a recipe from Darina Allen's Ballymaloe Cookery School in County Cork, Ireland, this delicious, hearty eye opener or dessert, is great in all seasons and especially in cold weather. You may enjoy this with a little cold heavy cream or milk spooned on top.

2	cups mixed unsulphered dried fruits (such as apples, pears, prunes or peaches)
1	cup unsulphered dried apricots
3	tart apples (such as Granny Smith, Macoun, or Mackintosh)
	Juice from ½ lemon
¼	cup honey
1	cup water
1	cup orange juice
2	tablespoons butter cut into bits

⑥ In a large mixing bowl, combine the dried fruits and the apricots with enough warm water to cover. Cover with plastic wrap and soak for 2 hours or up to overnight in refrigerator.

⑥ At cooking time, peel, core, quarter and thinly slice the apples; place in a separate bowl with the lemon juice and enough water to cover. Set aside.

⑥ Preheat the oven to 375°. In a medium bowl, stir together the honey, water, and orange juice.

⑥ Drain the liquid from the dried fruits and from the apples, combining together in a 4-quart baking dish.

⑥ Pour the orange juice mixture over the fruit. Stir to combine. Dot with butter. Cover the baking dish with a tight-fitting lid and bake in the oven for 35 minutes or until the fruit is tender. Remove from the oven and allow to cool for 5 to 10 minutes before serving.

Individual Baked Eggs Florentine

Yield: 2 servings

Some of our favorite variations of this dish include sundried tomato and Parmesan cheese, chopped ham and Cheddar cheese, steamed asparagus tips and sautéed vidalia onion. Let your imagination be your guide here. Use about 2 tablespoons of any filling combination for each serving.

5	ounces frozen spinach
4	ounces quality Swiss cheese
4	eggs
2	teaspoons butter
4	tablespoons heavy cream or half-and-half
	Salt and pepper

⑥ Prepare the spinach according to package directions. Drain in a fine sieve, pressing on the spinach with the back of a wooden spoon to extract as much of the liquid as possible; set aside.

⑥ Grate the Swiss cheese using the largest holes on a hand grater. Set aside.

⑥ Preheat the oven to 350°. For each serving: butter a 1-cup ramekin using 1 teaspoon butter. Spoon in 2 tablespoons chopped spinach. Break 2 eggs over the top of the spinach, followed by 2 ounces of grated Swiss cheese, and 2 tablespoons of the half-and-half or heavy cream. Season with salt and pepper. Repeat for the second serving.

⑥ Place the ramekins in a baking dish. Pour enough hot water into the dish around the ramekins to come about half way up the sides. Bake for about 15 minutes or until the eggs are cooked to taste. Serve in the ramekin.

Pumpkin Raisin Cake

Yield: one cake, 8 to 10 servings

A family recipe from our friend Bonnie Pizzorno, this is delicious for breakfast, but it makes a great special treat for teatime too.

4	eggs
2	cups sugar
1½	cups canned pumpkin puree
1½	cups flavorless vegetable oil
3	cups unbleached all purpose flour
2	teaspoons baking powder
2	teaspoons baking soda
2	teaspoons ground cinnamon
1	teaspoon salt
1	cup raisins
½	cup chopped walnuts

◐ Preheat the oven to 325°. Grease a 10-inch tube pan.

◐ In the bowl of an electric mixer fitted with the paddle attachment, mix together the eggs and sugar. Add the pumpkin and the oil; stir until well blended.

◐ In a separate bowl, stir together the flour, baking powder, baking soda, cinnamon and salt. Add to the egg mixture; mix well. Fold in the raisins and the chopped walnuts.

◐ Pour the batter into the prepared pan and bake in the oven for 1 hour or until a toothpick inserted in the center comes clean.

Whole Grain Irish Soda Bread

Yield: 2 loaves

Another variation of Irish soda bread, this one has the delicious flavor of whole grains and a wonderful moist texture.

2	cups whole-wheat flour
1	cup unbleached, all purpose flour
1	cup old-fashioned rolled oats
1	cup wheat germ
2½	teaspoons baking soda
1½	teaspoons salt
1	tablespoon granulated brown sugar
1½	cups raisins
2	tablespoons caraway seeds
2	cups plus ¼ cup buttermilk
2	tablespoons flavorless vegetable oil

⑥ Preheat the oven to 400°. In a large bowl, mix together the dry ingredients. Stir in the raisins and the caraway seeds.

⑥ Make a well in the center of the dry ingredients and add 2 cups of buttermilk and the oil. Stir together to combine and form a wet dough.

⑥ Turn the dough out onto a lightly floured work surface and knead about 3 minutes, adding additional flour if necessary, to prevent sticking.

⑥ Divide the dough into 2 equal portions. Shape each half into a round loaf and arrange on a floured baking sheet. Score a cross into the top of each loaf. Using a pastry brush, coat each loaf with some of the reserved ¼ cup buttermilk. Bake for 45 to 50 minutes or until golden brown and hollow sounding when the bottom of the loaves are tapped.

Winter Menu III

Poached Pears with Cranberry-Maple Sauce

Cinnamon French Toast with Caramelized Bananas

Poached Pears
with Cranberry-Maple Sauce

Yield: *10 servings*

Easy and elegant, this pear dish makes a splendid dessert. Serve one pear as a breakfast starter. Any pear will do but choose pears that are fragrant and free of blemishes.

12	ounces fresh whole cranberries
½	cup sugar
1	cup water
10	ripe pears, peeled
2	cups orange juice
½	cup pure maple syrup
2	tablespoons butter, cut into bits
¼	cup chopped pecans
10	orange slices, cut in half

❧ In a medium saucepan, combine the cranberries with the sugar and water. Bring to a boil, then simmer for about 15 minutes until cranberries begin to pop and the sauce thickens. Remove the sauce from the heat and reserve.

❧ Preheat the oven to 350°. Cut the pears in half, removing cores and stems. Place the pears, cut side up, in a baking pan large enough to hold them in one layer (to prevent browning).

❧ In a small bowl combine the orange juice and maple syrup. Pour the mixture over the pears, basting so that each fruit is fully moistened with the cooking liquid. Dot with butter.

❧ Bake the pears for approximately 30 minutes, or until tender, but not falling apart, basting 2 or 3 times during cooking. (Cooking time will vary slightly depending on the ripeness of the pears.) Remove from the oven.

❧ Measure out 1 cup of the orange-maple cooking liquid. Add ½ cup of the liquid to the reserved cranberry sauce and return the sauce to a simmer for 5 minutes, stirring to incorporate orange-maple mixture. Add more of the reserved liquid to the cranberry mixture if needed to create a medium-thick sauce.

To Serve:

❧ For each serving, ladle 2 ounces of the cranberry-orange sauce onto a plate, spreading the sauce out into a pool on the plate. Use 2 pear halves per serving and arrange them side-by-side, cut side down, on the sauce. Garnish with 1 teaspoon of chopped pecans and 2 half orange slices.

Cinnamon French Toast
with Caramelized Bananas

Yield: 5 servings

Our guests love this fruit-topped version of an old favorite. We usually serve it with crispy bacon or ham and offer pure maple syrup.

5	tablespoons butter
2	ripe bananas, peeled and sliced
1	tablespoon granulated brown sugar
¼	cup chopped walnuts
1	loaf (10 slices) day-old Challah bread or French baguette cut into 1-inch thick slices
10	eggs
1	cup milk
½	cup honey
2	tablespoons cinnamon
	Powdered sugar for garnish

⑥ Melt 1 tablespoon of butter in a medium skillet. Add the banana slices, sugar, and chopped walnuts. Sauté over medium heat for five minutes; set aside.

⑥ In a large mixing bowl, combine the eggs, milk, honey, and the cinnamon. Whisk to combine.

⑥ Poke holes in each bread slice with a fork and soak the slices in the batter for 1 minute, turning on both sides to thoroughly coat each slice.

⑥ Melt 2 tablespoons of the butter in a 10-inch skillet and add half of the bread slices. Do not crowd the pan. Sauté bread over medium heat on each side until browned. Add additional butter to the pan as needed until all bread slices are cooked.

⑥ For each serving: Reheat the caramelized bananas. Place 2 slices of french toast on a plate and spoon some of the fruit on top. Sprinkle with powdered sugar.

Notes

Dining in the Hamptons: Entrées

Alison by the Beach Restaurant in Sagaponack

Dining in the Hamptons: Entrées

One of the things that makes Eastern Long Island so special is the variety and quality of our many restaurants. In addition to savoring the beaches and parks and taking in the gorgeous vistas, visitors to the Hamptons have the opportunity to enjoy some of the finest foods and wines available anywhere. We have invited the chefs from twelve of the many excellent eating establishments in the Hamptons to contribute a special entree, in many instances featuring local ingredients. This selection of entrees is merely a small sample of the many culinary treats awaiting you the next time you visit the area. Try these yourself, and when you visit don't miss the opportunity to sample more at any of these fine restaurants.

Roasted Halibut
with Wild Mushroom Sauce

Yield: 2 servings

*Contributed by Chef Kevin Penner of **Della Femina Restaurant** in East Hampton, New York (516) 329-6666. Owned by ad-man Jerry Della Femina, Della Femina is the only restaurant in East Hampton with a three-star rating from The <u>New York Times</u> and <u>Newsday</u>. Serve this house specialty with your own favorite mashed potatoes. We love it with a Long Island Chardonnay. Wild mushrooms such as hedgehogs or chanterelles can be purchased at specialty grocers. White truffle oil can be mail-ordered through specialty food companies such as Dean and Deluca in New York City at (212) 226-6800.*

2	tablespoons olive oil
2	(7-ounce) Halibut loin pieces
	Salt and pepper to taste
5	tablespoons sweet butter, cut into ½-inch pieces
2	cups chanterelle or hedgehog mushrooms
1½	cups chicken stock (homemade or canned)
1	tablespoon coarsely chopped fresh thyme
2	tablespoons white truffle oil

⑥ Preheat the oven to 450°. Heat the 2 tablespoons of olive oil over medium heat in a 12-inch oven-proof sauté pan. Season the halibut with salt and pepper. Add the fish to the pan after the oil has almost begun to smoke. Cook on one side until it is browned; turn the fish over and place in the oven for 6 to 7 minutes depending on the thickness of the fillets, until cooked through. Remove from the oven and reserve.

⑥ In a 4-quart saucepan, melt 2 tablespoons of the butter over medium heat, add the mushrooms and cook until wilted. Add the chicken stock, salt and pepper to taste and the thyme. Reduce the heat to low and add the remaining 3 tablespoons of butter 1 piece at a time, stirring until each piece is dissolved before adding the next piece. Cook and stir until the sauce thickens slightly (a few minutes).

⑥ Remove the fish from the pan. For each serving, place a piece of fish on a dinner plate, spoon half of the mushroom sauce over and around the fish. Drizzle with 1 tablespoon of truffle oil. Repeat with the second portion.

Roasted Swordfish with a Red Lentil Crust and Lemon-Thyme Sauce

Yield: 4 servings

*Contributed by Chef John Yashinowsky of **Caswells Restaurant** in Montauk, New York; (516) 668-0303. Caswells features new American cuisine in a light and airy setting opening onto the Atlantic Ocean. Specialties of the house feature local seafood, produce and Long Island wines. Chef Yashinowsky accompanies this dish with Potatoes Anna and the freshest pencil thin asparagus briefly cooked in boiling water to tenderize them. An unusual aspect of this dish is the use of ground red lentils to coat the fish before cooking. Serve with a Chardonnay wine such as Tabott or SagPond.*

Potatoes Anna:

3	russet potatoes, peeled
¼	cup (½ stick) butter
1	small onion, cut into small dice and sautéed
	Kosher salt and freshly ground pepper

Fish:

4	(7-ounce) pieces swordfish (2.5-by-2.5 inches)
½	cup ground red lentils (use a coffee bean grinder)
	Kosher salt and freshly ground pepper
¼	cup (½ stick) butter

Lemon Thyme sauce:

¾	cup white wine
1	large shallot, finely chopped
½	cup fish stock or bottled clam juice
½	cup (1 stick) cold unsalted butter, cut into cubes
2	tablespoons coarsely chopped fresh thyme
2	tablespoons finely chopped fresh parsley
	Juice of 1 lemon
4	whole thyme sprigs for garnish

Asparagus:

1	pound fresh pencil-thin asparagus, blanched in boiling water for 1 minute.

To prepare potatoes:

ᕼ Slice the potatoes into ⅛-inch thick slices; stack the slices (do not put in water).

ᕼ Preheat the oven to 400°. Heat a 10-inch ovenproof sauté pan over medium heat and add the butter. Start making a spiral with the potato slices, starting in the middle of the pan and overlapping each

(*Roasted Swordfish continued*)

potato slice by half. When the bottom spiral is complete, sprinkle all of the sautéed onions on top and season with salt and pepper to taste. Make a top spiral layer, again starting in the middle of the pan. Cook until golden brown on the bottom, then flip the potatoes over and place the pan in the oven for about 8 minutes or until cooked through. (The potatoes can be made a few hours in advance and reheated in the same pan until crisp and golden brown).

To prepare fish:

- Preheat the oven to 400°. Heat a 10-inch ovenproof sauté pan over medium heat. Add the butter to the pan. Season the swordfish with salt and pepper and press 1 side of the fish into the ground red lentils.

- Cook the swordfish lentil-side down for about 2 minutes, being careful not to brown the lentils too much. Turn the fish over and place the pan into the oven for 8 to 10 minutes.

- Remove the swordfish from the pan and hold, covered in a warm place while making the sauce.

To prepare sauce:

- Pour the wine and the shallots into a saucepan and cook over medium heat. Let the wine reduce by half, then add the fish stock and reduce by half again. Turn off the heat and whisk in the cold cubed butter, the chopped thyme, parsley and the lemon juice. Season with salt and pepper to taste.

To serve:

- Divide the sauce evenly between 4 dinner plates and place one piece of fish on each plate on top of the sauce. Cut the reheated potatoes into quarters and place one piece on each plate. Divide the blanched asparagus evenly between the 4 plates and garnish with fresh thyme sprigs.

Saffron Risotto with Asparagus and Mussels

Yield: 4 servings

*Contributed by Chef Joseph Realmuto of **Nick and Toni's Restaurant** in East Hampton, New York; (516) 324-3550. Nick and Toni's is an extremely popular and elegant restaurant showcasing not only the best local food products, but also an extensive collection of artwork. The menu features an eclectic Mediterranean style with Tuscan and Provençal accents. The restaurant serves a variety of dishes using local and organic products whenever available including those from their own ½-acre organic garden behind the restaurant.*

Mussels:

3	tablespoons olive oil
⅓	cup chopped shallots
4	cloves garlic, peeled and crushed
3	dozen cultivated mussels, washed and debearded
1	cup white wine

Asparagus:

4	quarts salted water
1	bunch thin asparagus

Risotto:

5	cups chicken broth (fresh or canned)
⅛	teaspoon saffron or turmeric
1	tablespoon olive oil
2	cloves garlic, chopped
½	cup minced shallots
1	pound Arborio rice
½	cup dry white wine
4	tablespoons butter
1	sprig thyme, chopped
	Kosher salt
	Ground pepper

To prepare the mussels:

⑥ In a large pot, heat the oil over medium heat. Add the shallots and garlic, cook for about 5 minutes. Add the mussels and wine. Boil over high heat (covered) until the mussels open (about 5 minutes). Remove the mussels and reserve the liquid to make the risotto.

To prepare the asparagus:

⑥ Bring the water to a boil. Add the asparagus to the water. Cook until crisp-tender, about 3 minutes. Strain the asparagus and refresh under cold water. Cut into 1-inch pieces. Set aside.

(*Saffron Risotto continued*)

To prepare the risotto:

ↄ In a large saucepan, combine the reserved mussel stock with the chicken broth and the saffron. Bring to a boil and reduce heat to a simmer.

ↄ In a heavy bottom saucepan, heat the oil and add the garlic and shallots. Cook, stirring frequently over low heat, for 5 minutes, until softened but not brown. Add the rice. Stir the mixture constantly for 5 minutes. Add the wine and cook until almost completely absorbed (keep stirring). Add the simmering stock 1 cup at a time, stirring constantly, until each cup is absorbed. Stop when the rice is cooked through but still slightly firm; this whole process takes about 15 to 20 minutes. Stir in the 4 tablespoons of butter. Add the reserved mussels and asparagus, continue cooking just to heat through. Transfer to bowls, garnish with chopped thyme. Season with salt and pepper, serve immediately.

Salmon Cakes

Yield: 24 cakes

Contributed by Chef Dennis MacNeil of **Peconic Coast Restaurant,** East Hampton, New York (516) 324-6772. Peconic Coast serves a variety of delicious foods in a casual setting. In addition to a fine selection of seafood, Chef MacNeil prepares a divine roast chicken with sage, sautéed calves liver with seedless grapes, tarragon, vermouth and rice pilaf and the best mashed potatoes. Don't miss it if you are visiting the area. This recipe is done in several steps. The béchamel sauce, which is a classic white sauce, needs to be made in advance as it is used chilled to make the salmon cakes. A roux is a thickening agent made with cooked flour and butter. It is used here to thicken the béchamel sauce.

Béchamel sauce:

2½	cups milk (Do not use fat free)
½	small onion, peeled and stuck with 2 whole cloves
1	clove garlic, crushed
2	sprigs fresh thyme
1	bay leaf
¼	teaspoon ground nutmeg
	Salt and white pepper
1½	cups (3 sticks) butter
¾	cup all-purpose flour

Saffron garlic sauce:

½	cup dry white wine
1	teaspoon Spanish saffron or turmeric
1	tablespoon minced garlic
2	cups prepared mayonnaise
	Salt and pepper

Salmon cakes:

1	cup chilled béchamel sauce
1	whole egg
1	egg yolk
2	stalks celery, finely chopped
3	shallots, minced
4	tablespoons fresh lemon juice
1	tablespoon Dijon-style mustard
¼	teaspoon salt
	Freshly ground black pepper to taste
11	ounces smoked salmon, coarsely chopped
21	ounces fresh salmon, boneless fillet, coarsely chopped
¾	cup unseasoned bread crumbs
4	tablespoons (½ stick) butter, melted
2	lemons, each cut into six wedges for garnish

(Salmon Cakes continued)

Béchamel Sauce:

⑥ In a medium saucepan, combine the milk, onion, garlic, thyme, bay leaf, nutmeg, salt and pepper. Cook over medium heat until the milk begins to foam around the edges of the pan. Remove from the heat and set aside while making a roux.

⑥ In a separate medium saucepan, melt the butter over low heat. Add the flour and mix into the butter with a wooden spoon. Cook over very low heat for about 5 to 6 minutes stirring continuously. The roux should remain light in color, do not let the flour brown. (If the mixture gets too hot during the cooking time it will burn.) If necessary, remove the pan from the heat for a few seconds to cool it off before proceeding. Remove the finished roux from the heat and set aside.

⑥ Strain the milk to remove all of the solids. Return the flour mixture to low heat and add the strained milk to it. Cook over a low flame whisking continuously for about 5 minutes to remove any lumps. Continue to cook for about 12 to 15 minutes at a simmer whisking occasionally. Remove from the heat and strain the finished sauce through a fine sieve into a bowl and refrigerate.

Saffron garlic sauce:

⑥ In a small mixing bowl, combine the white wine, saffron and garlic. Allow to infuse for 30 minutes.

⑥ In a separate medium mixing bowl, combine the mayonnaise with the wine mixture and whisk well to combine. Add salt and pepper to taste and set aside in the refrigerator until serving time.

Salmon cakes:

⑥ Preheat the oven to 350°. In a large mixing bowl, combine the chilled béchamel sauce, whole egg, egg yolk, celery, shallots, lemon juice and mustard. Season with salt and pepper. Stir to combine.

⑥ Fold in the smoked and fresh salmon to form a loose but homogenous mixture. Form the mixture into 24 3-ounce cakes about 1-inch thick.

⑥ Gently pat each cake in the breadcrumbs to coat on all sides. Using a pastry brush, brush both sides of each cake with some butter and arrange on nonstick baking sheets. Bake in the oven for 8 to 10 minutes turning the cakes over once during the cooking time. Serve 2 cakes per portion with some of the saffron garlic sauce and garnish each portion with a lemon wedge.

Amagansett Lobster Sauce with Sweet Corn and Fettuccine

Yield: 4 servings

Contributed by Chef Colin Ambrose of **Estia Restaurant** *in Amagansett, New York; (516) 267-6320. Chef Ambrose notes that fresh pasta, though not required for this dish, matches the luxurious nature of the lobster and is highly recommended. This special dish shows off some of Amagansett's best assets: corn, peppers, cilantro, parsley, carrots, and leeks from local gardens and fresh lobster from Gardiner's Bay. Each of the elements of this recipe can be prepared up to 5 hours in advance of serving. Fresh pasta is Estia's claim to fame and the foundation of their menu. The restaurant takes pride in offering the freshest products possible. This particular dish is best served with a salad of crisp, spicy greens in a light vinaigrette with a bottle of Chardonnay from any one of Long Island's fine vineyards.*

7	tablespoons salt
3	1½ pound lobsters
3	cups chicken stock
4	large leeks
4	stalks celery
4	carrots
4	large cloves garlic, finely minced
4	ears of corn
½	bunch parsley
¼	bunch cilantro
8	plum tomatoes, blanched, skin and seeds removed and each cut into eighths
2	jalapeño peppers, seeded and finely diced
1	1-inch piece fresh ginger, peeled and minced
1	cup dry white wine
½	cup (1 stick) unsalted butter
1	pound fresh uncooked fettuccine

To prepare the lobster:

❧ Fill a 6-quart saucepan with water and bring to a rolling boil. Add 4 tablespoons of the salt to the water and submerge the lobsters. Cover the pot and boil the lobsters for 4 minutes. Remove the lobsters and submerge them in ice water immediately. (At this point, the lobster may seem slightly undercooked, which is fine since they will be heated again.)

❧ When the lobsters are cool, crack the shells and remove all of the meat making sure to keep the claw meat intact. (The shells are the key to true lobster flavor in the sauce, so save them all.) Discard only the roe and innards; set the lobster aside in the refrigerator.

To prepare vegetables:

❧ Clean the leeks by slicing the white part from top to bottom lengthwise and rinsing each layer thoroughly under running water to remove the sand.

⑥ Coarsely chop 1 piece each of celery, carrot, and leek. Combine with 1 piece of minced garlic in a bowl and set aside to make the lobster stock.

⑥ Cut all of the kernels off the corn cobs, saving the kernels in a bowl. Reserve the cobs.

⑥ Thinly slice the remaining leeks into match-stick size pieces about 2-inches long, using the majority of the leek except for the top ⅓. Cut the remaining carrots and celery in the same manner.

⑥ Remove the stems from the parsley and cilantro and rinse the leaves thoroughly under cold running water. Chop the leaves and reserve on a paper towel to remove any excess moisture.

To prepare stock:

⑥ Preheat the oven to 375°. Place all of the lobster shells and corn cobs in a medium roasting pan and place in the oven for ½ hour. Remove from the oven and reserve. Meanwhile, in a large saucepan heat ¼ cup butter over medium heat. Add the reserved coarsely chopped stock vegetables. Stir the vegetables until they begin to soften, then add the roasted lobster shells and corn cobs; the chicken stock and the white wine. Bring to a boil over high heat, then lower to medium heat and cook for 45 minutes.

⑥ In a medium saucepan, melt the remaining ¼ cup butter over medium heat and add the remaining garlic, jalapeño, and ginger. Cook for 1 minute. Add all of the match-stick vegetables and stir. Increase the heat to high and cook for 5 minutes. Reserve the vegetables in a separate bowl and reserve the unwashed saucepan for reducing the stock.

⑥ Using a strainer lined with cheesecloth, strain the lobster stock into the reserved saucepan and return to the stove top. Cook over medium heat until the stock is reduced to about 3 cups.

Assembly of sauce:

⑥ Put a large saucepan of water on to boil for the pasta. In a medium saucepan, add the reserved stock and match-stick vegetables, bring to a boil over medium heat. Add the reserved corn kernels, the diced tomatoes and the lobster meat, except for the claws. Boil for 1 minute and remove from the heat. Stir in the parsley and the cilantro. Pour ½ cup of the stock into a separate small bowl and immerse the claw meat to heat it up. (This will be used as a garnish.)

⑥ When the pasta water is at a full boil, add the remaining 3 tablespoons of salt. Add ½ of the pasta and cook for 2 minutes. Remove the pasta with tongs reserving the water to boil the remaining pasta. Add the cooked pasta to the lobster sauce, stir gently to combine. Cook the other half of the pasta in the same water for 2 minutes. Add to the sauce and stir gently again to fully combine the ingredients and coat the pasta with the sauce. Divide evenly among 4 bowls and garnish with the lobster claws.

Horseradish-Crusted Salmon with Beet Risotto and Mustard-Glazed Cippolini Onions

Yield: 4 servings

Contributed by chef Raymond Higgins of **The Farmhouse Restaurant** *in East Hampton, New York; (516) 324-8585. Built in the late 1600's, this dining room was the home and center of a 55 acre East Hampton working farm. The restaurant uses fresh organic produce and takes pride in its hearty portions, local fish and fowl combined with a creative kitchen. The philosophy of this restaurant is simple, they want you to have a terrific experience. Although this recipe has several steps, it is easy to prepare and makes a grand impression. Cipollini onions are the small bittersweet bulbs of the grape hyacinth and look like small onions. Cippolinis are not easy to find and are only in season in the fall. Some Italian markets may be able to supply you. You may substitute small pearl onions if you cannot locate them.*

Beet Risotto:

20	large beets, large stalks cut and removed
4	tablespoons unsalted butter
2	tablespoons finely chopped shallots
	Salt and pepper to taste
1	pound Italian Arborio rice
2	cups red wine
3	tablespoons finely chopped parsley

Mustard-glazed cippolini onions:

2	tablespoons vegetable oil
1	tablespoon unsalted butter
16	peeled cippolini onions
	Salt and pepper to taste
½	teaspoon turmeric
2	tablespoons Dijon-style mustard
¾	cup dry white wine

Horseradish crust:

½	cup (1 stick) unsalted butter, softened
¼	cup prepared horseradish
1	teaspoon Worcestershire sauce
1	teaspoon lemon juice
¼	cup finely chopped parsley
½	teaspoon onion powder
½	teaspoon garlic powder
¼	cup dry white wine
	Salt and pepper
½	cup unseasoned breadcrumbs

(*Horseradish-Crusted Salmon continued*)

Chive beurre blanc:

½	cup dry white wine
1	tablespoon finely chopped shallots
6	whole peppercorns
2	bay leaves
½	teaspoon white wine vinegar
½	cup heavy cream
1	cup (2 sticks) unsalted butter
	Juice of ½ lemon
¼	cup finely chopped chives
	Salt and pepper

Salmon:

	Salt and pepper
4	(7-ounce) salmon fillets, skinless and boneless
¼	cup vegetable oil
1	tablespoon unsalted butter

To prepare beet risotto:

ⓖ In a medium saucepan, boil 1 large beet until done (45 to 60 minutes). Remove the beet from the water and allow to cool completely, then peel and dice it; set aside.

ⓖ Juice the remaining beets in a vegetable juicer. Skim the foam off the top of the beet juice and discard the foam along with the pulp; set juice aside.

ⓖ In a large saucepan, heat 2 tablespoons of the butter over a medium heat; add the shallots and cook and stir for 3 minutes. Add the salt and pepper, and the rice, stirring the rice constantly. Add 1 cup of the red wine and continue stirring. When the liquid is absorbed, add the remaining 1 cup of wine and continue stirring. When the rest of the liquid is absorbed, add ½ of the beet juice and continue to stir until absorbed, then add the remaining beet juice. When most of the liquid is gone, remove the rice from the pan and spread it out on a cookie sheet and allow it to cool. Set aside.

To prepare onions:

ⓖ Heat the oil and the butter in a large sauté pan. Add the onions, salt and pepper, turmeric, and mustard. Stir the onions well and add the white wine. Bring to a boil and then simmer the onions for 8 to 10 minutes. Remove the onions from the liquid with a slotted spoon; set aside and let cool.

To prepare crust:

ⓖ In the bowl of a food processor fitted with a steel blade, combine the butter, horseradish, Worcestershire sauce, lemon juice, parsley, onion powder, garlic powder and the white wine. Season

(*Horseradish-Crusted Salmon continued on next page*)

(*Horseradish-Crusted Salmon continued*)

with the salt and pepper and pulse to combine. Add the breadcrumbs and pulse again to form a paste. Remove from the food processor and set aside.

To prepare chive beurre blanc:

- In a non-reactive saucepan, combine the wine, shallots, peppercorns, bay leaves, and vinegar. Bring to a boil and reduce to about ¼ cup of liquid. Strain through a fine sieve and return the liquid to the same pan. Add the cream, and cook over low heat until reduced by half.

- Lower the heat to a simmer and whisk in the butter 2 tablespoons at a time completely dissolving the butter before adding more. (If the sauce gets too hot it will break.) If necessary, remove the pan from the heat for a few seconds to cool it down before proceeding. When all of the butter has been added, turn off the heat and add the lemon juice and chives. Season with salt and pepper.

- Strain the sauce through a fine sieve into a metal mixing bowl. Set the bowl over a pot of simmering water to keep it warm while cooking the fish.

To prepare salmon:

- Preheat the oven to 450°. Season the salmon fillets with salt and pepper.

- In a large sauté pan, heat the oil until very hot, then add the butter.

- Carefully place the salmon in the pan, flesh-side down. Cook for 3 minutes, until the salmon is browned. Turn the salmon over and cook the other side for 1 minute. Remove from the pan and let cool.

- When the salmon is cool, spread a thin coat of the horseradish paste across the top of each fillet, covering the entire fillet; set aside on a cookie sheet.

Assembly:

- In a large saucepan, bring 1 cup of water to a boil. Add the reserved rice.

- Place the salmon and the onions in the preheated oven and cook for 5 to 6 minutes, until the salmon is cooked to your taste and the onions are heated through.

- As the rice is being stirred, add the reserved diced beets, the remaining 2 tablespoons of butter and the chopped parsley. Cook until the water is absorbed and the rice is cooked through but still slightly firm.

- Divide the risotto evenly between 4 dinner plates. Put 4 onions around each plate. Place 1 salmon fillet on top of each bed of risotto. Reheat the chive beurre blanc sauce over low heat, being careful not to break the sauce. Drizzle about ¼ cup of the sauce onto each salmon fillet.

CASWELL'S

Located at the tip of Long Island in Montauk, Caswell's
specializes in such fine seafood dishes as Roasted Swordfish with a Red Lentil
Crust and Lemon-Thyme Sauce.

MILL HOUSE INN, HAMPTON BREEZES ROOM
A private start to the day at the Mill House Inn includes Brie and Fresh Herb Omelet Spirals and Strawberry Rhubarb Compote.

NICK AND TONI'S

Dine with the cognoscenti at the world famous Nick and Toni's Restaurant in East Hampton and enjoy Saffron Risotto with Asparagus and Mussels.

CHRISTMAS AT THE MILL HOUSE INN
A romantic Christmas breakfast at the Mill House Inn featuring Poached Pears with Cranberry Maple Sauce and French Toast with Caramelized Bananas.

FARMHOUSE

Horseradish-Crusted Salmon with Beet Risotto and Mustard-Glazed Cippolini
Onions is just one of many fine dishes served at the charming
Farmhouse Restaurant in East Hampton.

PECONIC COAST

Chef Dennis MacNeil at Peconic Coast in East Hampton serves up delicious Salmon Cakes with Saffron Garlic Mayonnaise.

DELLA FEMINA
See the stars in caricature at Della Femina's in East Hampton and enjoy Roasted Halibut with Wild Mushroom Sauce.

ESTIA
Fresh pasta combined with local produce and a sublime lobster sauce is the signature dish of Estia Restaurant in Amagansett.

Oysters on the Half Shell with Gingered Granité

Yield: 4 servings

*Contributed by Chef Rick Jakobson of **Alison by the Beach Restaurant** in Sagaponak, New York; (516) 537-7100. Owned by Alison Hurt, who also owns Alison's on Dominick Street in Manhattan, the food at Alison by the Beach has been described by the food writer of the local weekly newspaper the* East Hampton Star *as " a really outstanding meal that you couldn't achieve in your home in your wildest dreams". Each course and each wine achieving near perfection. Here is a sample of the chef's genius in taking simple ingredients and creating sublime flavor. The unusual twist here is the use of a granité or flavored ice as the accompaniment to fresh oysters. A granité is created by combining water, sugar and either a sweet or savory liquid flavoring. The characteristic granular texture of the granité is achieved during the freezing process by occasionally stirring the mixture with a fork to break up the ice crystals. The granité needs to be made at least 3 hours ahead of when you plan to serve the oysters.*

Simple syrup:

½   cup granulated sugar
½   cup water

Gingered Granité:

1¼   cups rice wine vinegar
4   tablespoons finely chopped shallots
1   tablespoon grated fresh ginger
2   teaspoons whole black peppercorns, crushed

Oysters:

16   oysters, shucked right before serving time

To prepare syrup:

In a small saucepan, bring the sugar and the water to a boil; let cool and set aside.

To prepare granité:

Mix the rice wine vinegar, simple syrup, shallots, ginger, and peppercorns. Pour into a 13-by 9-by 2-inch glass baking pan and place in the freezer for about 3 hours or until frozen. Stir occasionally with a fork to break up the ice crystals. When frozen, stir again to break up the granité. Transfer to a freezer-friendly container and store in the freezer until ready to use.

For each serving:

Arrange 4 of the shucked oysters on a plate. Spoon some of the granité over the oysters and serve immediately.

Pan Seared Tuna with Sautéed Yukon Gold Potatoes, Black Grapes and French Radishes over Mizuna Salad

Yield: 6 servings

Contributed by Chef Gretchen Menser of **Rowdy Hall Restaurant** in East Hampton, New York; (516) 324-8555. Rowdy Hall takes its name from a turn-of-the-century boarding house in East Hampton. Local folklore has it that the boarding house would fill with artists and writers visiting the East End. There, during the wee hours of the night the residents would eat and drink and generally raise a ruckus. Hence the name "Rowdy" was christened. Today Rowdy Hall is a bistro/pub using fresh local ingredients where one can enjoy a great burger and a pint or a dish such as this one and a glass of wine.

Use the freshest possible Yellowfin or Big Eye tuna. Ingredients such as Yukon Gold potatoes, black grapes and french radishes, if not available at the local market, can be purchased at specialty stores. White balsamic vinegar is also available at specialty stores and local farmer's markets. Serve with Sagpond Domaine Wolferer 1994 and a nice crispy baguette.

Sautéed Yukon Gold Potatoes:

6	Yukon Gold potatoes
2	tablespoons olive oil
1	teaspoon salt
1	bunch french radishes, sliced in half (may substitute regular radishes)
1	medium bunch seedless black grapes, sliced in half
¼	tablespoon chopped fresh rosemary
¼	tablespoon chopped fresh thyme
¼	tablespoon chopped fresh parsley
1	ounce white balsamic vinegar
¼	cup (½ stick) unsalted butter

Salad:

1	pound Japanese mizuna lettuce (may substitute arugula or mesclun mix)
¼	cup extra virgin olive oil
1	bunch fresh chives, finely chopped

Pan Seared Tuna:

6	7- to 8-ounce Yellowfin or Big Eye tuna steaks, 1½-inches thick
	Salt and freshly ground black pepper
2	tablespoons olive oil

(*Pan Seared Tuna continued*)

To prepare potatoes:

⑥ Wash the potatoes and place them in saucepan. Cover with cold water and add the salt. Boil until just tender. Remove the potatoes and allow them to cool. When cool, cut into a medium dice.

⑥ Heat 2 tablespoons of olive oil in a 8-inch heavy-gauge sauté pan over medium high heat; add the potatoes, sauté until brown; add the radishes, sauté 1 minute; add the grapes, sauté 1 minute; add the fresh chopped rosemary, thyme, and parsley.

⑥ Add the white balsamic vinegar. Reduce the heat and add the butter; stir constantly until the mixture thickens.

To prepare salad:

⑥ In a stainless steel bowl, combine the mizuna with the finely chopped chives and olive oil. Season with salt and fresh ground pepper.

To prepare tuna:

⑥ Preheat the oven to 500°. Season the tuna steaks with salt and freshly ground pepper, set aside.

⑥ Heat 2 tablespoons of the olive oil in a 10-inch heavy-gauge sauté pan or cast iron pan over high heat. Sear the tuna on all sides until brown. Place the tuna on a cookie sheet and bake in the oven for 5 to 10 minutes or until cooked medium rare, remove and put aside.

For each serving:

⑥ Place some of the salad mixture on a dinner plate; slice 1 portion of tuna in half and place both halves over the salad. Spoon some of the potato-grape-and-radish mixture over the tuna. Repeat with the remaining servings.

Grilled Vegetable Quesadillas

Yield: 2 (10-inch) round quesadillas

Contributed by Chef Stanley Singer of **Turtle Crossing Restaurant** *in East Hampton, New York; (516) 324-7166. Noted for its "slow-cooked, fall-off-the-bone barbecue, Turtle Crossing is a barbecue "joint" featuring western regional cooking from Texas, Oklahoma, California and Mexico. We especially love the quesadillas and the tortilla wraps with a variety of fillings such as Blackened Mango Salmon or the grilled fresh vegetables featured here. Serve this with your favorite Mexican-style salsa, guacamole and sour cream.*

Curry-Cumin vinaigrette:

⅓-½	cup fresh lemon juice
1	teaspoon curry powder
½	teaspoon cumin powder
¼	teaspoon ground ginger
3	teaspoons coarsely chopped cilantro
1	teaspoon minced garlic
¼	teaspoon salt
½	teaspoon dry mustard
½	teaspoon freshly ground pepper
½	teaspoon sugar
⅔	cup vegetable oil

Quesadilla:

1	small yellow squash, cut into ¼-inch-thick rounds
1	small zucchini, cut into ¼-inch-thick rounds
1	small fennel, cleaned, outer stalks removed and cut into quarters
1	small red bell pepper, cut in half, seeds removed and sliced into ½-inch strips
1	small red onion, peeled and quartered
1	small carrot, cut into ⅛-inch rounds
¼	cup olive oil
4	(10-inch) flour tortillas
2	cups shredded smoked Gouda cheese
1	tablespoon butter, melted

To prepare the vinaigrette:

⚄ Combine all of the ingredients for the vinaigrette, (except the vegetable oil) in a medium sized bowl. Whisk vigorously, slowly adding the oil to emulsify. Set the vinaigrette aside.

To prepare the quesadillas:

⚄ Toss the prepared vegetables in ¼ cup of olive oil and grill or broil until cooked al dente.

(*Grilled Vegetable Quesadillas continued*)

⑥ For each quesadilla: Brush 1 flour tortilla on one side with the melted butter; place the butter side down in a 12-inch sauté pan over low heat. Top with ½ of the shredded Gouda and ½ of the grilled vegetables. Drizzle with 2 tablespoons of the vinaigrette. Top with the second tortilla and brush with the butter. Press together to seal. Cook until the underside is browned and the cheese begins to melt. To cook second side, slide quesadilla out of the pan onto a dinner-plate. Invert the sauté pan over the quesadilla, holding the plate and pan together. Flip the pan back over so that the uncooked side of the quesadilla is now in the pan. Cook until the second side is browned. Remove from the pan and cut the quesadilla into 8 wedges. Repeat for the second quesadilla.

Seared North Atlantic Salmon with Chive Potato Blinis and Brussels Sprouts

Yield: 4 servings

Contributed by Chef Robert Rawleigh of **The Laundry Restaurant** in East Hampton, New York (516) 324-3199. **The Laundry Restaurant** features classic American cuisine balanced with contemporary dishes, keeping the restaurant familiar yet vibrant. The dining room staff compliments the inviting warmth of the signature fireplace with caring professional service. Established 18 years ago, The Laundry always provides an enjoyable dining room experience.

Blinis:

1	pound peeled white potatoes, cut into 1-inch dice
2	teaspoons salt
¼	cup whole milk
4	tablespoons all-purpose flour
3	tablespoons extra-virgin olive oil
3	large eggs
3	large egg whites
1	tablespoon finely chopped chives
½	teaspoon ground nutmeg
	Ground pepper
	Coarse sea salt

Fish:

2	pounds fresh salmon fillets cut into 4 equal pieces
2	tablespoons olive oil
	Salt and pepper

Butter sauce:

1	cup fish stock (or substitute bottled clam juice)
1	cup (2 sticks) butter, cut into 1-inch pieces
	Lemon juice from 2 lemons
2	tablespoons chopped fresh thyme
	Salt and pepper to taste

Vegetable:

2	pounds Brussels Sprouts, thinly sliced into rounds
4	teaspoons poppy seeds
1	tablespoon butter
	Salt and pepper

(*Seared North Atlantic Salmon continued*)

Garnish:

4   chives, finely chopped

To prepare the blinis:

๖ Place the potatoes in a medium-sized saucepan. Add enough cold water to cover and 2 teaspoons of salt. Bring the potatoes to a boil, then simmer until tender. Drain the potatoes well, return to a large warm bowl and mash well with a potato masher. Mix in the milk, flour and 2 tablespoons of the olive oil. When everything is well incorporated beat in the whole eggs.

๖ In a separate medium mixing bowl, beat the egg whites to a soft peak. Fold the egg whites and the chives into the potato mixture; season with nutmeg, coarse salt and fresh ground pepper to taste. Cover and set aside.

๖ Heat the remaining 1 tablespoon of olive oil in a 12-inch sauté pan. Spoon 2 ounces of the blini batter into the pan for each blini. Do not crowd the pan. Cook the blinis over medium heat until golden brown (approximately 1 minute). Flip each blini over and cook on the second side until medium brown in color. Repeat until all of the batter is used. Set aside and keep warm.

To prepare butter sauce:

๖ In a medium-sized saucepan, bring the fish stock or clam juice to a boil and reduce over medium high heat for 1 to 2 minutes. Reduce the heat to low and add the cold butter 2 pieces at a time whisking well after each addition. (If the mixture gets too hot the sauce will break). Remove the pan briefly from the heat to cool it down if necessary before adding the next bit of butter. Season with lemon juice, thyme, salt and pepper.

To prepare fish:

๖ Preheat the oven to 400°. Heat 1 tablespoon of the olive oil in a nonstick ovenproof 12-inch sauté pan. When it is just smoking, add the salmon fillets to the pan. Cook 1 to 2 minutes on medium-high heat, flip over and put in the oven for 3 to 4 minutes until cooked medium.

To prepare Brussels Sprouts:

๖ In a medium sauté pan, melt the 1 tablespoon of butter over medium high heat. Sauté the brussels sprouts until crisp tender. Add the poppy seeds and season with salt and pepper.

To Serve:

๖ Arrange a salmon fillet in the center of 4 warm plates. Evenly divide the reserved blinis and the Brussels sprouts among the four plates. Reheat the butter sauce over a low flame, then drizzle some sauce around each plate and garnish each serving with chopped chives.

Light Tuscan Fusilli with Herb-Crusted Tofu

Yield: 10 servings

Contributed by Chef Daniel Van Der Beek, **Babette's Restaurant,** *East Hampton, New York; (516) 329-5377. Babette's is a vegetarian restaurant and juice bar; also serving fish and poultry, always with an innovative twist. Chef Van Der Beek has created some unique dishes such as Tempeh Fajitas, Portobello Jerky and a popular BBQ Tofu. This pasta dish features the chef's use of soy and tofu to a create a heavy cream-like sauce that is completely dairy free.*

Steamed vegetables:

1	bunch broccoli; florets only
½	head cauliflower; florets only
1	cup fresh or frozen green beans, trimmed and halved
1	cup baby carrots; split in half lengthwise

Pasta:

1	teaspoon salt
1	tablespoon olive oil
1	pound dry fusilli

Soy cream base:

½	block extra-firm tofu
1	cup plain (unflavored) soy milk
2	heaping tablespoons raw cashew butter
2	small cubes vegetable bouillon
1	teaspoon onion powder
½	teaspoon garlic powder

Pesto:

1	cup raw cashew pieces
2	heaping tablespoons nutritional yeast
1	bunch fresh basil leaves; washed, stems removed, dried and coarsely chopped
¾	cup olive oil
2	cloves garlic coarsely chopped
½	teaspoon fresh lemon juice
¾	teaspoon sea salt
4	drops hot red pepper sauce or ¼ teaspoon white pepper

(*Light Tuscan Fusilli continued*)

Herb crusted tofu:

2	tablespoons unbleached all purpose flour
1	tablespoon granulated onion (not powder)
1	tablespoon granulated garlic
½	tablespoon dry mustard
1	tablespoon dry basil
1	teaspoon whole dry thyme
1½	teaspoons sea salt
1½	teaspoons sugar
2	quarts water
2	teaspoons lemon juice
1½	blocks extra firm tofu cut into ½-inch cubes
⅓	cup canola oil

Assembly:

2	tablespoons olive oil
6	cloves fresh garlic finely chopped
2	small zucchini; quartered lengthwise and cut into ½-inch thick diagonals
2	small yellow squash; quartered lengthwise and cut into ½-inch thick diagonals
1	red bell pepper; seeded, cut lengthwise into ¼-inch strips
3	Portobello mushrooms, stems removed, and cut into ½-inch strips
¼	teaspoon crushed red pepper flakes (optional)
1	teaspoon sea salt
4	small fresh tomatoes cored and cut into a medium dice
1	bunch scallions trimmed and thinly sliced crosswise

To prepare vegetables:

৬ In a large saucepan or stock pot, bring enough water to the boil to cover the broccoli, cauliflower, green beans and carrots.

৬ When the water boils, add the vegetables and blanch for 3 to 4 minutes until they are crisp-tender. Immediately remove from the heat, reserve 1 cup of the cooking liquid.

৬ Transfer the vegetables to a strainer, discarding the rest of the liquid, and refresh the vegetables with cold water to stop the cooking process. Set aside.

To prepare pasta:

৬ In a large saucepan, bring enough water to a boil to accommodate the fusilli. Add the salt and the olive oil, then the pasta. Cook the fusilli until it is al dente. Drain the pasta, refresh with cold water and reserve.

(*Light Tuscan Fusilli continued on next page*)

(*Light Tuscan Fusilli continued*)

To prepare soy base:

ⓑ In a blender combine all of the cream base ingredients and blend until smooth, stopping once or twice to scrape down the ingredients from the sides of the blender to ensure even mixing. Reserve refrigerated until ready to use.

To prepare pesto:

ⓑ In the bowl of a food processor fitted with a metal blade, process cashews and yeast until smooth, about 3 minutes. Remove from processor and reserve in a medium mixing bowl.

ⓑ In the same unwashed processor bowl, combine the basil, olive oil, garlic, lemon juice, salt, and pepper. Blend until smooth.

ⓑ Mix basil mixture into reserved cashew mixture and set aside in the refrigerator

To prepare herb-crusted tofu:

ⓑ Make the herb flour: In a 1-gallon plastic food bag or a medium mixing bowl, combine the flour, onion, garlic, mustard, basil, thyme, salt, and sugar.

ⓑ In a 4-quart saucepan, bring the water and the lemon juice to a boil. Reduce the heat, add the tofu cubes and simmer for 10 minutes. Pour the tofu into a strainer and allow it to drain and air-dry for 5 minutes, shaking occasionally to remove excess water. Transfer tofu to a cookie sheet lined with paper towels and pat the tofu dry.

ⓑ Heat the canola oil in a large sauté pan over medium-high heat. Transfer the dried tofu to the flour mix and either shake or stir gently to coat evenly. Remove the tofu from the flour and sauté it in the oil tossing gently until evenly browned. Remove the tofu from the pan with a slotted spoon and drain on paper towels to remove as much oil as possible.

Assembly:

ⓑ In a large saucepan, heat the olive oil over medium heat. Add the garlic and stir for 30 seconds; do not allow to burn. Add the zucchini, yellow squash, red pepper, and mushrooms. Cook for 5 minutes, or until crisp-tender.

ⓑ Add the reserved broccoli, cauliflower, green beans and carrots. Cook for 1 minute.

ⓑ Add the reserved cream base, the pesto and the reserved 1 cup of vegetable cooking liquid. Reduce the heat to low. Stir to combine and simmer gently for 1 to 2 minutes to heat through.

ⓑ Add the reserved fusilli, the herb crusted tofu and toss gently. Simmer over a low flame to heat through and serve.

Trinette Pasta with Lobster, Grilled Corn, Saffron and Basil

Yield: 4 servings

Contributed by Chef Ricardo Traslavina of **95 School Street** in Bridgehampton, New York; (516) 537-5555. A casual, yet elegant atmosphere, **95 School Street** serves regional cuisine highlighting the foods and wines of Eastern Long Island. This sublime pasta dish, featuring several of our best local ingredients, originated when chef Traslavina's pasta supplier came to him with a unique problem. He told the chef that many of his clients were suddenly requesting lasagna noodles without the curly edges. He had been cutting them off and was now left with pounds of seemingly unusable lasagna curls. He wondered if Chef Traslavina could invent a dish using these 'left overs'. The chef agreed, purchased the lasagna curls for a nominal fee, and using his knowledge of local ingredients, came up with a great summer pasta dish. Feel free to substitute fusilli, mafalda or another curly pasta for the Trinette.

4	live lobsters (1-1½ pounds each)
4	ears fresh corn, husk on
6	ounces dry white wine
1	medium onion, coarsely chopped
1	carrot, coarsely chopped
2	stalks celery, coarsely chopped
1	bay leaf
1	sprig fresh thyme
1	sprig fresh parsley
¼	cup heavy cream
¼	teaspoon saffron
	Salt and pepper
1	pound Trinette pasta
2	plum tomatoes, diced
2	teaspoons fresh basil, finely chopped
2	teaspoons butter

⑥ Boil enough water in a deep stock pot large enough to hold the lobsters. Immerse the lobsters and simmer for 3 minutes. Place the lobsters in ice water for a maximum of 5 minutes. Remove the lobsters from their shells. Reserve the shells. Chill the lobster meat in the refrigerator.

⑥ Grill or roast the corn, Remove the husk and cut the kernels from the cob. Set aside.

⑥ In a medium stock pot, combine the lobster shells, white wine, onions, carrots, celery, bay leaf, thyme, and parsley. Add enough water to cover the shells. Bring to a boil and simmer for 10 minutes. Strain the stock, reserving the liquid.

⑥ In a medium saucepan combine the reserved stock with the cream and the saffron. Season with salt and pepper. Return to a boil and simmer to reduce the stock down to 4 cups of liquid.

⑥ In a large pot, cook the pasta as directed on the package until al dente. Drain the pasta, returning it to the cooking pot. Add the stock mixture along with the diced tomatoes, reserved lobster meat, corn and the basil. Stir in the 2 teaspoons of butter. Reheat to serve.

Notes

Wolffer

1994

The Hamptons, Long Island

ESTATE SELECTION
CHARDONNAY

ESTATE BOTTLED BY SAGPOND VINEYARDS

SAGAPONACK, NEW YORK, USA • ALC. 13.5% BY VOL. • 750 ML

As a native Long Islander and wine lover, I've always wanted to support our local wine industry. The idea of consuming a wonderful beverage produced in our own backyard is extremely appealing. Having a home-grown, handmade fine wine would certainly provide us with a great source of pride and perhaps entitle us to some dignified bragging rights. As I started sampling various wines by the handful of producers in the early to mid 1980's, I was at first very pleased with what I tasted, and then disappointed, then pleased, then disappointed. The consistency, or lack of, was a serious concern. Disillusioned by what I experienced, I stopped drinking Long Island wines. As eager as I was to support the local wine industry, I just didn't want to shell out the bucks on a product of varying quality.

It was perhaps five or six years later before I again tasted a Long Island wine. I was the wine director for a restaurant in midtown Manhattan when I reluctantly agreed to see a wine sales rep from one of the Long Island wineries, as a favor to a mutual friend. The sales rep brought along the wine maker and we tasted the wines. WOW! These wines were a far cry from what I remembered tasting a few years before. I bought the wine for the restaurant and was simultaneously resurrected as a champion of Long Island wine. This sales rep later invited me to the annual Long Island Barrel Tasting as her and the winery's guest. All of the Long Island wineries were in attendance showcasing their 1995 merlots out of barrel. She introduced me to the various wine makers and winery owners. I tasted the wines, all of them, twice. Consistency was no longer an issue.

This is an incredibly exciting time to be involved in the wine industry on Long Island. While Europe is the old grand-daddy of viticulture areas and California is approaching adolescence, Long Island is growing from its infancy into a toddler. The changes are rapid. From an industry that has just recently begun, to the development and progress that has transpired in a mere twenty-five years, it's an amazing life process to witness and to some extent (at least on the periphery) participate in. The beautiful part of this "happening" is that anybody can join in on the fun and excitement. Raise a glass of fine Long Island wine and you're in the loop.

France has had centuries to develop their knowledge of where each grape variety is best planted (a notion the French termed 'terroir,' that we have since adopted). California, in the true American spirit, researched and developed technology in the vineyard and winery to make the best wine scientifically. Meanwhile, eastern Long Island, for the most part, was cultivating potatoes. Europe has since employed many of the technological advances made in the laboratories and applied them to their own vineyards and wine making practices. The California and other 'New World' wine regions have learned to better understand terroir and the time honored traditions and wine making techniques of the wines they hold up as the benchmarks of world class wine. Long Island has been able to take advantage of this recent global evolution of wine resulting in a geometric progression of quality.

Students of wine know that climate is the most critical factor of fine wine production. Soil, drainage, sun exposure and air flow (breezes) are also extremely important. Long Island wine country happens to be blessed with the best of all of these criteria. Our maritime influenced climate provides the temperate environment ideal for fine wine production.

The oceans, bays and Long Island Sound regulate temperature fluctuations by holding heat to help eliminate the risk of frost. The temperature difference between these bodies of water and the air creates breezes which help keep grapes dry and therefore minimizes rot. A relatively long and cool growing season allows grapes to stay on the vine longer and develop character. The fair amount of sun filled days ensures ripening. Our soil composition allows for proper drainage yet provides adequate moisture retention. Eastern Long Island is situated perfectly to produce world class wine…and does!

Long Island wines stylistically fall somewhere between the opulence of the fruit driven California wines and the austerity of the 'Old World' (French) wines. The common characteristic amongst our wines is acid. Acid gives a wine vitality. It allows wine to age gracefully, developing a greater depth of flavor and subtle complexity. Acid also makes a wine partner well with food. Think of a squeeze of lemon on fresh fish and how it livens your palate. Wine heightens the flavors of food thus elevating the entire dining experience. Long Island wines by and large are great food wines. There are also several simpler wines produced here which are wonderful on their own or paired with easy meals; be sure to try these as well.

When exploring all that Long Island wines have to offer, you may want to take a few moments to ponder the attributes of each wine. As in all other pursuits, the more you know about the subject at hand, the greater the potential for appreciation.

First, look at the wine. Is it red, white, rosé or sparkling? Now that you have determined the color, look a little closer and determine the hue. This is best done in a well-lit area and by tilting the glass of wine against a white background for examination. Holding a glass of wine in the air will not reveal its true color as it takes on the tones of whatever background may be present.

If the wine is red, is the color more towards purple, indicating a younger wine, or is it tawny and fading at the edges, perhaps showing some age? If the wine is white, is it a pale straw color or is it more golden, once again indicating an older wine. As a rule, white wine gains color with age while red wine loses color. Both eventually will turn brownish, indicating that the wine is past its prime. Is your red wine opaque, indicating a highly extracted or bigger style wine or is it translucent, maybe denoting a lighter bodied wine? Fuller bodied wines, both red and white, generally show more intensity in their color while lighter bodied wines will, logically, show less depth of color. Is the wine clear and bright or is it cloudy and murky? Which would you prefer to drink?

Smell the wine. Does it smell like fruit or does it smell more vinous or wine-like? Are there any off-putting odors or is it clean? Does the wine remind you of any other familiar smells? Perhaps certain fruits, herbs, vanilla, butterscotch, honey, spice, smokiness or toast come to mind. Someone once said a particular wine reminded him of roast beef. This is a perfectly acceptable descriptor. Taste is subjective and is therefore in the palate of the beholder.

Taste the wine (this is the fun part). Take a generous sip, more than a tiny drop or two and less than a mouthful. Roll the wine around in your mouth making sure it comes into contact with all parts of your tongue. You can chew the wine, gargle it, aerate it by sucking in and making funny bubbling noises, whatever works for you. As long as you find some way to extract as much flavor as the wine has to offer.

Do you sense any sweetness on the top of your tongue? Does your tongue tingle along the sides, indicating the presence of acid? Is there any bitterness towards the back of your tongue? Do you feel the sensation of heat in your throat, displaying a high alcohol presence in the wine? How was the mouth-feel of the wine? Was it coating, rich and luscious or was it clean, refreshing and crisp? Is the taste still with you? For how long? Did it dissipate immediately? Now you must swallow or spit, a no brainer decision if nothing is planned for the remainder of the day that requires the operation of heavy machinery.

Using a format when tasting wine, however casual or formal, will enhance your enjoyment of the beverage. Reading about wine will bolster your wine geek vocabulary by providing certain buzz words. Practicing wine tasting will help you understand and identify with the terminology associated with wine analysis and descriptions.

If you're like me, the food you choose to eat is determined by the wine you've begun to drink. However, realizing that most of us prefer to determine the food first and then select a wine, I have these basic guidelines to offer.

The old school of thought is to match red wine with red meat and white wine with fish and white meat. A more recent approach suggests that you drink what you like regardless of what you eat. There is merit to both. Keeping this in mind, let's make up some rules.

1. **Drink what you like.** Otherwise, what's the point? A 'classic' food and wine pairing won't do you any good if you don't like the wine. Exposing yourself to and analyzing the different flavor and textural components of wines will enable you to form opinions as to what you like. Armed with your preferred flavor profile, a good wine shop will be able to suggest a variety of wines that meet your criteria. As you begin to understand your palate and appreciate wine, you will naturally become more adventurous in selecting new wines to try.

2. **Compliment or contrast.** Birds of a feather…Bold flavored foods generally work well with bold wine. Simple rustic wines with simple country foods. Elegant wine with more refined cuisine. Opposites do attract. Think of Chinese sweet and sour dishes, why do they work well? Off dry (slightly sweet) wines pair well with spicy foods.

3. **High acid, low alcohol.** Acid is the backbone of wine. On its own, a wine may drink well, but when paired with food it becomes flat, flabby, dull and unexciting. This occurs when the wine is low in acid and cannot stand up to the richness of the food. Alcohol in wine will accentuate well seasoned, spicy food. If the wine is high in alcohol, the wine will become hot, bitter and harsh on the palate and in the back of the throat. Therefore, the best food wines are high in acid and low in alcohol.

4. **Red wine, red meat.** Red wine has tannic acid, white wine does not (well, very little anyway). Tannic acid, or tannin is the life blood of red wine. It is also present in other familiar items such as tea or aspirin. It is this component in these products that makes your mouth pucker, that kind of tart drying feeling on your gums. Adding milk (fat) to tea rounds out and smooths over the tannins, just as the fat in a juicy grilled sirloin steak affects that tannic red wine. A wine with little or no tannin will not be able to stand up to the flavors in the steak. Lower fat meats can, logically, pair with less tannic wines. Red wines with little tannin can work well with fish and poultry. Big styled wines can work well with low fat meats.

Long Island wines offer something for everybody. We have simple everyday wines, elegantly structured wines ideal for cellaring and styles that run the gamut. On the following pages we offer you an overview of the South Fork and North Fork wineries as a guide to your tasting tour of the East End. As the world discovers our wines, it is good to know that we can have confidence, be proud and brag…with dignity.

Robert Fairbrother
General Manager, Laundry Restaurant
President, Long Island Chapter of the Sommelier Society of America
East Hampton, New York
May, 1998

A Tour of the Wineries
The South Fork Wineries

Channing Daughters, 1927 Scuttlehole Road, Bridgehampton, 537-7224
Named after the four children of Walter and Molly Channing, the winery of Channing Daughters was set to open to the public in the summer of 1998. Mr. Channing has been growing grapes since 1982, starting out as an experiment. Thoughts of getting into the wine business began 10 years later, as Mr. Channing explored ways to preserve some of the undeveloped land he had amassed off Scuttlehole Road in Bridgehampton by using it for alternative agricultural purposes with economic promise. Beginning in 1994, Mr. Channing started having wine made especially for him, and two years later he decided to make his wines available to the public and build his own winery.

Inspiration for his vineyard also came from Mr. Channing's ties to France: His mother, though American, was reared in France, and he maintains friendships in that country that provide advice on the craft and business of wine-making. With his wife, Mr. Channing owns 125 acres off Scuttlehole Road (his home is just a short distance away from the winery), almost half of which are woods and 15 acres of which (formerly potato fields) are planted with vines.

Channing Daughters' first two wines, a 1996 chardonnay and a 1995 merlot, were produced by North Fork wineries, the white at Peconic Bay Vineyards in Cutchogue and the red at Lenz Winery in Peconic. (More information on those can be found in following pages.) But with his own winery complete, Mr. Channing was looking forward to producing his own chardonnay and merlot on premises. Plantings of pinot gris and Lemberger will insure other offerings in the future of the youngest of the East End wineries.

The winery is aiming to appeal not necessarily to oenophiles but to ordinary people. "We're most interested in people who like to enjoy wine instead of being overly serious about it," Larry Perrine, Channing Daughters' winemaker and general manager, told a local newspaper. Those "overly serious," he said, are people "who worry about what score a wine got in a wine magazine or a wine competition." Tastings were sure to be a central part of the new winery building.

Channing Daughters' labels reflect another passion of Mr. Channing's-wooden sculpture concentrating on the intriguing root systems of trees, a spare and almost spooky look that resembles bare grape vines. Several of his sculptures grace the winery property. By profession, Mr. Channing is involved in venture capital investing for start-up businesses in the medical field.

Duck Walk Vineyards, Montauk Highway, Water Mill, 726-7555
Duck Walk Vineyards' owner, Dr. Herodotus Damianos, known affectionately as Dr. Dan, got his start with a North Fork winery he still owns and operates, Pindar Vineyards. (More information on Pindar can be found in the following pages.) Some 56 acres at Duck Walk are planted with 32,000 vines, bearing pinot gris, early and July muscat, black Alexander, pinot meunier, merlot, and chardonnay grapes. Some varietals were planted for the first time on Long Island.

Duck Walk began in 1994, when Dr. Damianos, a Stony Brook University Medical Center internist, bought the former Le Reve Winery. The inspiration for the name Duck Walk is twofold. Part comes from Long Island duckling, a recognizable and world-renowned culinary delicacy. The other part, comes from the fact that, back in the 1930s and '40s, the land adjacent to the vineyards was home to a poultry and duck farm. Hence, the vines now flourish where, once, ducks walked.

Like many others in the winery business on the East End, Dr. Damianos also sees vineyards as a way to preserve the area's agricultural character, which he says "is necessary for all our well-being." And, he takes pride in being responsible for the largest single planting of vinifera grapes in Southampton Town's agricultural history, more than 350 years.

Over the years Duck Walk Vineyards has garnered numerous awards for its products, made under the tutelage of its winemaker, Mark Friszolowski. They include a double gold medal for its Aphrodite late harvest gewurztraminer at the San Francisco Fair International Wine Competition, a gold medal for its merlot at the New York State Commercial Wine Competition, another gold for its 1994 reserve merlot at the San Diego National Wine Competition, a gold medal for its cabernet sauvignon in the Dallas Morning News National Wine Competition, and a silver medal for its reserve chardonnay at a recent New York State Fair.

The 11,000-square-foot Normandy chateau-style winery building is a familiar site for those who travel along Montauk Highway, the main road to the South Fork's easternmost communities. Tours and tastings are offered at Duck Walk, which also has a boutique of wine-related gifts, local crafts, and culinary accessories. And, on Saturday and Sunday afternoons in the summertime, Duck Walk features live music on its patio, overlooking the vineyards.

 **SAGPOND Vineyards,** 139 Sagg Road, Sagaponack, 537-5106.

The 50 acres of rolling hills that once yielded potatoes but today comprise SAGPOND Vineyards lie north of Montauk Highway in the hamlet of Sagaponack, just east of Bridgehampton. Founded in 1987 by Christian Wolffer, SAGPOND has now integrated, beginning with its 1996 vintage, all of its wines under one label-Wolffer.

The winemaking philosophy of Mr. Wolffer, SAGPOND, and the vineyards' well-respected winemaker, Roman Roth, is to combine old world techniques and artistry with state-of-the-art technology. Careful attention is paid to each vine as it grows in the field, and all grapes are hand-picked. The vineyard is dedicated to extensive canopy management as well as to limited yields for its reserve wines, although as a whole SAGPOND strives to grow and produce some of the world's most respected wines. SAGPOND grows chardonnay and Bordeaux varietals, including merlot, and lovingly, craftingly turns out a traditional Burgundy-style chardonnay, a rich merlot, and a dry rosé, as well as a pinot noir and a sparkling wine.

In the end SAGPOND's product is the result of a personal love of wines on the part of Mr. Wolffer, a world-traveled businessman who over 18 years bought 168 acres in Sagaponack, dedicating them not only to the vineyard but to a horse farm as well. "Someone once told me patience is at the heart of all great vineyards," Mr. Wolffer wrote after his vineyards' 1996 harvest. "It is only when a person completely understands this truth-that producing a great wine may never be achieved in one's lifetime-will they truly master the craft of superior winemaking."

Mr. Wolffer's and Mr. Roth's efforts have not gone unnoticed. <u>Wine Spectator</u> wrote of SAGPOND's 1994 Domaine Wolffer Chardonnay Reserve that it was "strongly marked by both rich oak, with toasty, butterscotch flavors, and bright citrusy acidity, this has character…" And, The <u>New York Times</u> wrote that "SAGPOND's basic, everyday chardonnay…is exceptionally light-bodied; it comes across in the peppy, refreshing way young chablis, sancerre, and muscadet does."

SAGPOND's 12,000-square-foot winery building, designed in the style of the grand European estate and completed in May 1997, is as beautiful as it is functional and makes for a great time for those interested in tastings and tours. SAGPOND also periodically offers educational seminars (it is the site of a 1998 course leading to a sommelier certificate, the first project of the new Long Island Chapter of the Sommelier Society of America) and is available for private and special events.

The North Fork Wineries

Bedell Cellars, Main Road (Route 25), Cutchogue, 734-7537.

Kip Bedell has garnered particular attention for the merlots he has produced at his winery, and they tend to sell out quickly. He made the only Long Island merlot to be rated outstanding by <u>Wine Spectator</u>, after all. Tours of the small operation are offered by appointment only, though the tasting room is said to be quite lively.

Bidwell Vineyards, Route 48, Cutchogue, 1-800-698-9463.

A family owned and operated estate winery, Bidwell Vineyards was established in 1982 and has 30 acres of the North Fork's fertile land under cultivation. Bidwell's philosophy is two-fold: That the North Fork produces unique and superior wine grapes reflected in the "singular style" of the wines, and that its wines should be known for their value as well as their quality. Bidwell's crops are crafted into sauvignon blanc, chardonnay, merlot, cabernet sauvignon, and white riesling wines. The winery offers free tastings and tours are available upon request.

Corey Creek, Route 25, Southold, 765-4168.

Owned by Joel and Peggy Lauber, Corey Creek Vineyards' 30 acres is nestled between Richmond and Corey Creeks, two fingerlike tidal inlets that form small pockets of year-round temperate climate. It produces limited edition wines with chardonnay, pinot noir, gewurztraminer, merlot, and cabernet franc vines planted. Corey Creek's tasting facilities were under construction when this book went to press, but are expected to open the summer of 1998.

Gristina Vineyards, 24385 Main Road (Route 25), Cutchogue, 734-7089.

In 1984, Jerry and Carol Gristina planted 30 acres of vines in this farming town, and Gristina Vineyards has been a family-run business ever since. In Mr. Gristina's words, his winery focuses on "adherence to strict viticultural techniques" in creating its vinous. Gristina continues to expand without sacrificing quality a bit, evidenced by the fact that it has been honored as a <u>Wine</u>

<u>Spectator</u> Critics' Choice. Free tastings are available in the tasting and sales room overlooking the trellised vines, which are split between chardonnay, merlot, cabernet sauvignon, cabernet franc, and pinot noir varieties. Tours are available by appointment only.

Hargrave Vineyard, North Country Road, Route 48, Cutchogue, 1-800-734-5158.

Hargrave Vineyard finds pride in being Long Island's first planted estate vineyard of European wine grapes since Colonial times. Since starting in 1973, it has grown to more than 2,000 acres, though at press time it was reported to be for sale by its owners, Alex and Louisa Hargrave. They planted exclusively old-European vinifera varieties, most notably the very first merlot to be planted this side of the Rocky Mountains, and follow the philosophy that "good wine is grown, not made."

Hargrave produces chardonnay, sauvignon blanc, pinot blanc, cabernet franc, and pinot noir. Among its many honors are numerous <u>Wine Spectator</u> Critics' Choice citations and being selected to accompany the food at impressive restaurants, such as the Four Seasons and Le Cirque and Les Dames d'Escoffier annual dinner. The winery offers free tastings although appointments are necessary for tours.

Jamesport Vineyards, Main Road, Jamesport, 722-5256.

The vines of this North Fork winery, owned by the Goerler family, were planted in 1981, and Jamesport Vineyards has been producing wines since 1989, "in the finest European tradition." Before that Ron Goerler Sr. and Jr. sold grapes from their vineyards at Early Rising Farm in Cutchogue to other winemakers. Forty acres of vines-bearing chardonnay, sauvignon blanc, merlot, cabernet sauvignon, pinot noir, riesling, cabernet franc, pinot blanc, and semillion-are planted on one of the highest elevations on the North Fork with a predominant southwest exposure, a setting that makes for quality, ripened fruit. Awards include three medals at the 1997 New York Wine & Food Classic, including a double gold for their 1995 late harvest riesling. Free tastings are poured in the Jamesport winery's tasting room, housed in a 150-year-old barn, and tours of the operation are available on weekends.

Laurel Lake Vineyards, 3165 Main Road, Laurel, 298-1420.

Laurel Lake Vineyards began when Mike McGoldrick bought the former San Andres vineyard in 1994. Its 13 acres of chardonnay grapes, on a 30-acre property, were planted in 1980. Laurel Lake's first few vintages of chardonnay were bottled at Palmer Vineyards, before its own winemaker, in its own winery, turned out a chardonnay, cabernet sauvignon, white table wine, and rosé of cabernet. And, in addition to Laurel Lake producing for its own label, other area vintners have bought its crops for their reserve chardonnays. The Colonial-style winery includes the production area, a wine shop, and a tasting room, and tours are offered.

Lenz Winery, Main Road (Route 25), Peconic, 734-6060.

Lenz Winery has 40 acres in production and is still growing with Peter and Deborah Carroll running the show. They took it over in 1989 from former restaurateurs Peter and Patricia Lenz, who founded the winery in 1983. Constant blind tastings pitting their wines against others from around the world are how the Carrolls and their winemaker, Eric Frey, keep on top of quality.

Tried-and-true chardonnays, newer sparkling wines, pinot blanc, and cabernet sauvignon are among Lenz's offerings, and free tastings flow in a funky old barn turned tasting room. It is reached by journeying along a wooden walkway between sheds (a take on the traditional New England covered bridge) into a courtyard with two old maples at the center. The building is entered by passing under an arbor that at summer's peak offers a shady refuge. Tours of Lenz Winery are happily given.

Macari Vineyards, 150 Bergen Avenue, Mattituck, 298-0100.

Macari Vineyards, with 120 of the property's 300 waterfront acres planted, debuted its winery to the public Memorial Day weekend 1998. Joseph Macari Jr. heads this family-owned winery, the first on Long Island to operate a computer-controlled harvester and one that prides itself in a strong connection to French winemaking traditions. Its first-year releases feature two styles of chardonnay, sauvignon blanc, rosé d'une nuit, and merlot, with a red blend expected in the following year. And the winery building, whose architecture invokes the spirit of Tuscany, offers tastings in a setting that features a stone and timber deck overlooking the vineyard.

Osprey's Dominion Vineyards, 44075 Main Road (Route 25), Peconic, 765-6188.

The name for this North Fork winery comes from the East End's growing population of ospreys, for which tall nests are often erected by local environmental groups to encourage their habitation here. The owners, Bud Koehler, Bill Tyree, and Bill Pollina have been growing grapes since 1982. Among their varieties are merlot, chardonnay, and cabernet sauvignon. Driving east on Route 25 you'll notice signs indicating two areas of Osprey's Dominion vines, before arriving at the winery and tasting room, where you can relax on the patio and gaze out at more vines.

There, tours are available on request, though visitors are made to feel welcome to explore the winery-with 30,000 gallons of stainless steel cooperage and 15,000 gallons of (French and American) small oak cooperage-on their own as well. For the summer of 1998, Osprey's Dominion planned a number of special events, including live music, a bird of prey show, and antique aerobatic flyovers that can make the winery a reasonable stop for the whole family.

Palmer Vineyards, 108 Route 48, Aquebogue, 722-WINE.

This winery began in 1983 when Robert Palmer-the head of New York's R. J. Palmer Inc., a national media buying firm-envisioned rows of vinifera wines growing where corn, potatoes, and pumpkins had flourished in the past. That year, he planted his first vines on the vineyard's 80 acres. Since first being released in 1987, Palmer wines began accumulating awards and in its first 10 years they amounted to 45 golds (including six double and two triple), 115 silvers, and numerous bronze citations. Now, Palmer wines are sold in 23 states, are hitting the European markets, and for five years were served on American Airlines' transcontinental first class business service.

Merlot, cabernet, and chardonnay are among the wines Palmer produces. The classically designed winery and tasting house was designed to resemble the original, weather-aged barn on the property on the outside, but inside it resembles an old English pub. Palmer offers plenty of special events, including annual festivals on the Fourth of July and Labor Day weekends, cooking demonstrations and book signings, and the like. Cheap Kool-Aid and hot dogs are often offered with the purchase of a glass of wine, making Palmer another feasible stop for the whole family, not to mention hay rides through the vineyards that are popular with kids of all ages. Self-guided tours are encouraged, and tastings are available with a charge for some, including a structured tasting flight of three comparable wines.

Paumanok Vineyards, Main Road (Route 25), Aquebogue, 722-8800.

Founded in 1983, this 77-acre estate is owned and operated by Ursula and Charles Massoud (he is the head of the Long Island Wine Council) and their three sons. "Born and raised in the Old World, wine has always been a part of our lives, and we continue the practice at Paumanok Vineyards," the Massouds say. Paumanok's premium vinifera vines yield chardonnay, Johannisberg Riesling, sauvignon blanc, chenin blanc, cabernet franc, merlot, and cabernet sauvignon grapes, and their dense planting (1,100 vines per acre) is said to make for more concentrated fruit and thus a higher-quality finished product.

The winery, a renovated turn-of-the-century barn, houses the tasting room where free samples are offered as well as the fermentation tanks and lab. A deck and the tasting room look out onto the expansive vineyard. Special events-like evenings of food, wine, and music-are planned throughout the year at Paumanok, which is amenable to hosting private parties, weddings, and such. Tours are available as well.

Peconic Bay Vineyards, Main Road (Route 25), Cutchogue, 734-7361.

Ray Blum established his Peconic Bay Vineyards in 1980 and since retiring in 1994 he has devoted all of his time and attention to it, serving as both proprietor and winemaker. A former air traffic controller on Long Island, he brings degrees in both horticulture and business as well as his self-described, hands-on approach to his winemaking venture. Fifty-seven acres of vineyards are planted with cabernet sauvignon, chardonnay, merlot, and riesling grapes, and part of his energy is being devoted to creating vineyard-designated wines according to soil types.

Mr. Blum's wines were first produced in 1984, at first by a neighboring winery, but since 1989 all stages have been performed at his winery. More than 20 national and international awards have been garnered by Mr. Blum's Burgundian-style chardonnays. Peconic Bay's winemaking operations are located where a converted farmhouse holds the wine storage and tasting room. Behind the building are 30 acres of vines, and tours are given by appointment.

Pellegrini Vineyards, 23005 Main Road (Route 25), Cutchogue, 734-4111.

Bob and Joyce Pellegrini first got their start in the business as partners in Gristina Vineyards in 1982, but it was in 1991 that they purchased the vineyard which bears their name. Their 28-acre vineyard is planted with chardonnay, merlot, petit verdot, cabernet sauvignon, and cabernet franc vines. The Pellegrini approach to winemaking? To combine Old World traditions with state-of-the-art technology. Their philosophy, shared with others, is that wine is made largely in the vineyard, and special attention is given to what's happening in the fields. And their winemaker, the Australian Russell Hearn, is particularly well-respected in his circles.

Tastings of Pellegrini's award-winning wines (The <u>New York Times</u> called Pellegrini's 1993 wines "the single best collection" of that year's excellent vintage) are freely poured in the tasting room of its 14,000-square-foot winery, overlooking the vineyard. The tasting room is joined by a trellised walkway to the production facility, where visitors can observe from balconies. A second-floor private tasting area is also available (in 1997 it was the site of the practical portion of the championship round of the Sommelier Society of America's master sommelier competition). Tours are happily given here, though visitors are welcome to explore by themselves as well.

Pindar Vineyards, Route 25, Peconic, 734-6200.

The first vineyard opened by Dr. Herodotus Damianos, Pindar Vineyards got its start in 1979 and almost 20 years later has grown to nearly 300 acres of vines. Fifteen varieties are grown by Pindar and turned into Proprietor's Blends, two different styles of chardonnay, cabernet sauvignon, merlot, champagnes, and port. Dr. Damianos and his team follow the philosophy of paying "attention to every detail in the vineyard, and a minimal amount of handling, and only the absolute necessary movement of the wines in the winemaking process."

Pindar has amassed hundreds of awards in national and international competitions, as well as much praise, over the years. Take for example its 1995 Mythology, a Bordeaux, which Bon Appetit magazine dubbed in 1997 "one of the top 50 wines of the world," or its 1994 cuvée rare champagne, which in the same year won a gold medal from the American Wine Society. Guided tours teaching visitors about the entire winemaking process are offered daily at Pindar, and free tastings are offered in its tasting room along a copper-covered bar. A pavilion at the vineyard is the site of many Pindar events throughout the year.

Pugliese Vineyards, Route 25, Cutchogue, 734-4057.

For generations before him, Ralph Pugliese's family made wine in Italy. After his father immigrated to New York from Naples and he was born, Mr. Pugliese's family continued to make wine, only in the basement of their Brooklyn home. Today, the amiable Mr. Pugliese, his wife Patricia, and their children continue the tradition, only on 50 acres of former potato fields in Cutchogue. "Keep it natural and simple" is the credo of Mr. Pugliese, who offers tours by appointment and is eager to share a glass of wine with a visitor.

Pugliese Vineyards was established in 1980. Its vines bear chardonnay, cabernet sauvignon, merlot, pinot noir, riesling, cabernet franc, zinfandel, Niagara, and gewurztraminer grapes, and among the wines it produces are champagne, port, and white port. Free tastings are offered in the winery building, a converted barn that sits next to a picturesque pond, rusty old fashioned gas pump, and arbor with several picnic tables underneath, plus the vineyards beyond. Notice the hand-painted champagne and port bottles, done with nail polish by Mrs. Pugliese, who is also happy to personalize any bottle and, incidentally, dislikes the taste of wine!

Ternhaven Cellars, 331 Front Street, Greenport, 477-8737.

Ternhaven Cellars is a boutique winery that opened in May 1998 in Greenport, an historic maritime village, where it produces and sells its Bordeaux-style red wines in a storefront setting. Owned by Harold Watts and Carole Donlin, its five acres of vineyards, again on former potato fields, are located in nearby Cutchogue and have been growing since 1987. Its first several vintages were produced at Pellegrini Vineyards for the Ternhaven label and Corey Creek Vineyards was selling its merlot, cabernet sauvignon, and claret blend, but Ternhaven is now taking care of all stages itself, starting with the 1997 vintage.

Mr. Watts, an economics professor at Columbia University and weekend resident of Greenport, has been a winemaking hobbyist for 20 years, creating homemade wines from a kit. He plans to retire soon and serve as Ternhaven's vintner. Ms. Donlin, who handles the marketing aspect of the business, has a weekend home in another North Fork hamlet, Mattituck.

How To Get There: Green signs help direct visitors to all area wineries, both on the North and South Forks, so keep an eye out for them. Consulting a map and calling ahead for directions, particularly for the North Fork wineries, is advisable. Calling ahead of time for hours of business is also recommended, as the nature of the entire East End is a seasonal one.

Finding the South Fork wineries is easiest. Starting from the west, head east on Route 27 and you'll first encounter Duck Walk Vineyards, located on the immediate north side of Montauk Highway in Water Mill. You can't miss it. A few miles east on the left hand side (just past a Hess gas station) you'll find Scuttlehole Road. Follow this road through South Fork farmfields for about six miles, until you come to Channing Daughters. It will be on the right hand side.

When leaving the driveway of Channing Daughters, turn right, then make another right at the end of the road, and this will take you back to the main highway and a set of traffic lights. Turn left at the lights and several miles down the road you'll come to another set of lights; turn left there, and SAGPOND Vineyards is located several hundred feet north of the highway.

As for the North Fork wineries, most are located on one of two main roads, and the fork itself can be reached by either driving from Sunrise Highway to Riverhead and starting from the west or taking the small ferries from North Haven to Shelter Island and Shelter Island to Greenport and then starting from the east.

From either direction, those green signs will direct you to the nearby wineries. In some places you'll be greeted by large signs exclaiming "Welcome to Long Island Wine Country." The majority of North Fork destinations are located on either Route 25 (often called Main Road) and Route 48 (often called Sound Avenue).

Michelle Napoli
Assistant Managing Editor
East Hampton Star

Cooking Classes in the Hamptons: Hors d'oeuvres

A Summer Cooking Class at the Mill House with Kristi Hood

Cooking Classes in the Hamptons

During the summer and autumn months we offer a series of cooking classes at the Mill House Inn taught by Chef Kristi Hood. Kristi has been a chef at the Quilted Giraffe Restaurant in Manhattan and an instructor at Peter Kump's New York Cooking School. Most recently she oversees her own private catering business as well as teaching our cooking classes.

Kristi brings a love of fine foods as well as an abundance of culinary knowledge to her teaching. In recent years her cooking class series has included holiday baking, preparing a holiday feast, a series of quick and easy summer meals and a class on preparing hors d'oeuvres.

We usually have a group of ten or twelve students preparing the various hors d'oeuvres and then enjoy a post-class cocktail party featuring a selection of Long Island wines. The hors d'oeuvres class is by far the most popular one we offer and so we decided to include a chapter of hors d'oeuvre recipes here. All of these snacks can be prepared in advance and frozen, to be reheated when needed. They are easy to prepare and look and taste spectacular. Our students and their guests love them. Try them for yourself and enjoy.

Persian Rub

Yield: 1 cup

The flavors of this spicy rub are indigenous to many regions of the Middle East. It makes a deliciously different coating for grilled meats and fish. Larger quantities will keep for months if stored in the freezer.

¼	cup sesame seeds
¼	cup shelled pistachios
¼	cup whole almonds
¼	cup dried oregano
1	tablespoon allspice
2	tablespoons curry powder
	Salt
1	tablespoon finely ground black pepper

Ⓖ Preheat the oven to 300°. Spread the seeds and nuts out on a cookie sheet and toast them until lightly browned and dry (about 5 to 8 minutes).

Ⓖ Allow the nuts and seeds to cool completely and then grind them in a food processor until quite fine, about the consistency of coarse meal. Add the remaining ingredients and pulse to blend.

Ⓖ Dip meats or fish in the mix just before grilling.

Cheddar-Basil Crackers

Yield: 24 crackers

These delicious cocktail morsels freeze beautifully for up to three months after they are baked. They are especially delicious when served with a glass of wine or champagne. The addition of the crispy rice cereal gives the crackers a surprising extra crunch.

8	ounces grated medium Cheddar cheese
½	cup (1 stick) butter, softened
½	teaspoon hot pepper sauce
1	teaspoon Dijon-style mustard
1	cup unbleached, all purpose flour
2	tablespoons chopped fresh basil or Italian parsley
1½	cups crispy rice cereal (optional)

Ⓖ In the bowl of an electric mixer fitted with the paddle attachment, mix the cheese and the butter with the hot pepper sauce and mustard until well combined. Blend in the flour and basil, then the cereal.

Ⓖ Preheat the oven to 350°. Grease 2 baking sheets. Shape the dough into 2-inch rounds and place them on prepared baking sheets. Flatten with the bottom of a floured glass. Bake in the oven for 15 minutes or until golden brown.

Miniature Chicken-and-Mushroom Puff Pastries

Yield: 3 dozen

A rich cocktail morsel, these can be prepared ahead of time and frozen for up to 2 months. Bake the hors d'oeuvres frozen in a 375° oven for about twenty minutes.

Filling:

4	tablespoons butter
1	tablespoon minced garlic
⅔	cup minced onion
1	pound ground chicken (or turkey)
⅔	cup sliced white mushrooms
1½	tablespoons chopped fresh thyme or 2 teaspoons dried thyme
¼	cup chicken broth
¾	cup heavy cream
½	cup chopped parsley
	Salt and pepper

Pastry:

2	pounds defrosted puff pastry sheets

Assembly:

1	egg
2	teaspoons water

ⓑ Melt the butter in a large skillet. Add the onion and garlic; cook until translucent. Add the ground chicken and cook through, breaking up any lumps, about 3 minutes.

ⓑ Add the mushrooms and thyme, cook until the mushrooms soften, (about 2 minutes). Add the broth and cream.

ⓑ Continue to cook over medium heat, reducing the filling until it thickens. Remove from the heat, add the parsley and season with salt and pepper. Allow to cool.

ⓑ Preheat the oven to 375°. On a lightly floured work surface, roll out a sheet of puff pastry ⅛-inch thick. Using a 2-inch round biscuit cutter, cut circles. (Two circles form a top and bottom for each hors d'oeuvre).

ⓑ In a small bowl whisk together the egg and the water to make a wash so that a glaze forms while baking.

(*Miniature Chicken-and-Mushroom Puff Pastries continued*)

🍥 For each hors d'oeuvre, brush 1 circle with the egg wash and place a teaspoonful of chicken filling in the center of the egg washed circle. Brush a second circle and place it over the filling, egg washed side down, pressing it firmly onto the bottom circle with your fingers. Seal the 2 rounds using the tines of a fork to make a decorative edge. Cut a small air vent into the top. Brush the top with egg wash. Repeat until all of the filling and pastry has been used. Bake in the oven for 20 minutes or until the pastries are a glazed golden brown.

Dry Spice Dip for Vegetables

Yield: 1 cup

This is a delicious, and low calorie, alternative to standard vegetable dips. We especially love it with carrots and red peppers, but try your own vegetable ideas.

⅓	cup sugar
1	tablespoon dried oregano
1	teaspoon dried sage
½	cup curry powder
1	teaspoon ground cumin
¼	teaspoon cayenne pepper
1	teaspoon kosher salt

🍥 Combine the sugar, oregano, sage, curry powder, cumin and cayenne pepper in a spice mill or coffee grinder. Whirl until ground to a fine powder.

🍥 Pour the mixture into a medium nonstick pan. Stir constantly over low heat for about 10 minutes, until lightly browned. Add the salt and stir to combine.

Empanadas with Fresh Corn and Aged Cheeses

Yield: 3 dozen

Empanada is a Spanish word meaning "baked in pastry." These miniature turnovers are delicious on their own or served with the fruit chutney recipe which follows. Masa harina is flour that is made from sun- or fire-dried corn kernels that have been cooked in limewater. It can be purchased by mail-order from Dean and Deluca in New York City at (212) 226-6800.

Pastry:

1	cup masa harina
1	cup boiling water
1	cup unbleached, all-purpose flour
1	teaspoon salt
1	teaspoon sugar
1	egg
2	tablespoons melted butter
⅓	cup grated Gouda or Edam cheese

Filling:

1½	cups fresh (or frozen) corn kernels
1	cup coarsely grated smoked Gouda or Edam cheese
⅓	cup chopped red bell pepper (¼- to ½-inch dice)
½	teaspoon finely chopped fresh jalapeño, seeds removed (optional)
¼	cup finely chopped red onion
3	tablespoons finely chopped cilantro
	Salt to taste

Egg wash:

1	egg
2	tablespoons water
3	cups flavorless vegetable oil for frying.

☙ In a small bowl, combine the masa harina with the water and allow to cool.

☙ Place the masa dough in the bowl of an electric mixer fitted with the paddle attachment. Add the flour, salt and sugar. Mix to combine. Add the egg, butter and lastly, the cheese.

☙ Turn the dough out onto a lightly floured work surface. Knead until smooth. Shape the dough into a disk. Wrap in plastic wrap and refrigerate for 30 minutes.

☙ Make the filling: In a medium mixing bowl combine the corn, cheese, red pepper, jalapeño, onion and cilantro. Stir to combine. Add salt to taste and set aside. In a small bowl, whisk together the egg and the water to make the egg wash.

(*Empanadas continued*)

⑥ Roll the chilled masa dough out to ⅛-inch thickness on a lightly floured board. Cut into rounds, using a 3-inch round cookie cutter. Brush each round with egg wash and place a teaspoonful of filling in the center of each. Fold over the edge to form a semicircle and press the edges together firmly with fingertips. Seal with the tines of a fork, creating a decorative edge.

⑥ Heat the oil in a heavy saucepan to hot (350-375°). Fry each empanada, turning as each side browns, about 3 to 4 minutes. Drain on paper towels and serve.

Southwestern Fruit Chutney Yield: 2½ to 3 cups

Although delicious when served with the corn and cheese empanadas, this spicy chutney also makes a wonderful spread when combined with softened cream cheese and served with bread or crackers. When working with the dried red chilies, taste the chutney frequently to determine if it has reached the desired degree of spiciness for your taste. When it does, remove the chilies from the chutney even if it has not finished cooking yet. Tamarind paste, is made from the fruit of a tree native to Asia and Northern Africa. When the pulp and seeds are dried they become extremely sour and are used in Middle Eastern cuisine the way lemon juice is used in Western cooking. Tamarind paste can be obtained by mail-order from Dean and Deluca in New York City at (212) 226-6800.

2	tablespoons butter or flavorless vegetable oil
1	teaspoon finely chopped fresh ginger
2	small sticks cinnamon
1	teaspoon cumin or coriander
1-2	fresh or dried red chilies
1	small onion, finely chopped
2	pounds any combination of apples, mangos, or pineapple-peeled and diced ¼-inch
2	tablespoons tamarind paste or ¼ cup lemon juice
¼-½	cup packed brown sugar

⑥ Heat the butter or oil in a saucepan and add the ginger, cinnamon, cumin, chilies and onion. Cook for 1 minute over medium heat, stirring constantly. Add the apples and other fruits and cover tightly for about 5 minutes.

⑥ Remove the lid and add the tamarind paste and the brown sugar. Simmer until thickened; cool before serving. The chutney will hold for a month if kept refrigerated.

Phyllo Purses with Pecans and Gorgonzola Cheese

Yield: 3 dozen

Phyllo dough is a ready-made flaky pastry dough that is available in the frozen food section of many supermarkets. The trick to working with phyllo is to work quickly and to keep the dough you are not using covered with a damp cloth. These hors d'oeuvres can be frozen for up to 3 months and baked frozen in a 350° oven for 20 minutes or until golden brown.

4	ounces Gorgonzola cheese
4	ounces Farmers cheese
1	large egg
2	tablespoons coarsely chopped fresh basil
¼	teaspoon cayenne pepper
3	tablespoons toasted pecans or walnuts, finely ground
3	tablespoons grated Parmesan cheese
8	tablespoons butter, melted
1	pound defrosted phyllo dough

⑥ Combine the Gorgonzola and Farmers cheese in a small mixing bowl. Add the egg and mix well. Stir in the basil and season with cayenne.

⑥ In a separate bowl, combine the nuts and Parmesan cheese. Set aside.

⑥ Unroll the phyllo dough and cover with a damp cloth. Remove 1 sheet; place on a work surface and brush evenly with melted butter. Sprinkle on a light layer of the nuts and cheese mixture. Place another sheet of phyllo over the first. Press it gently down, brush with butter and sprinkle with nuts. Add a third and fourth layer of phyllo sheets in the same manner. Be sure to keep the unused phyllo covered with the damp cloth.

⑥ Preheat the oven to 375°. Lightly butter 2 baking sheets. With a sharp knife or pastry cutter, cut the layers into 4-inch squares and place a teaspoon of the gorgonzola filling onto the center of each. Pinch up the sides of each square to form a purse.

⑥ Place the finished purses on the prepared baking sheets, brush with a little additional butter and sprinkle the tops with a little nut mixture. Bake in the oven for 10 minutes or until golden.

Baked Spiced Nuts

Yield: 1 pound

Kristi Hood, our cooking instructor nick-named these "devil's own nuts". When you taste their spicy crunch, you'll see why. The nuts can be stored in an airtight container for up to 2 weeks at room temperature or for 3 months in the freezer. Bake in a 200° oven to refresh them before serving.

2	tablespoons Worcestershire sauce
2	tablespoons soy sauce
2	cloves garlic, peeled and sliced
1	teaspoon salt
½	teaspoon ground hot pepper
¼	teaspoon cumin
¼	teaspoon ground black pepper
2	dashes hot pepper sauce (optional)
2	egg whites
1	pound dry-roasted, unsalted peanuts or blanched almonds

⑥ In a blender, combine the Worcestershire sauce, soy sauce, garlic, salt, ground hot pepper, cumin, black pepper and hot pepper sauce until smooth. Add the egg whites. Mix until just blended.

⑥ Place the nuts in a stainless mixing bowl and pour the sauce over them. Allow to marinate for 30 minutes. Preheat the oven to 250°. Lightly oil 2 baking sheets.

⑥ Drain the nuts and reserve the liquid. Spread the nuts on prepared baking sheets and bake for 10 minutes. Drizzle the reserved marinade over the nuts. Stir to coat them and bake until a glaze that forms is dry, about 15 minutes.

⑥ Turn off the oven and allow the nuts to dry with the door propped open.

Mushroom Squares in Sour Cream Pastry   Yield: 2½ dozen

This is an hors d'oeuvre in which a rich filling is encased in a pastry. The finished squares can be frozen for up to three months and baked frozen in a 350° oven for twenty minutes or until golden brown. Enjoy them with your favorite cocktail beverage.

Pastry:

1½	cups unbleached, all-purpose flour
½	teaspoon salt
¼	teaspoon baking powder
7	tablespoons cold, unsalted butter, cut into bits
1	egg yolk
⅓	cup sour cream

Filling:

3	cups button mushrooms
1	cup chopped onion
2	tablespoons butter
¼	cup unseasoned bread crumbs
2	tablespoons sour cream
2	tablespoons chicken broth
2	hard-boiled eggs, peeled and chopped
3	tablespoons fresh dill
	Salt and pepper

Egg wash:

1	egg
2	teaspoons water

⑥ Make the pastry: In the bowl of a food processor fitted with a metal blade, combine the flour, salt and baking powder. Pulse briefly to combine. Add the butter and pulse until the mixture resembles coarse meal.

⑥ In a separate bowl, beat together the egg yolk and sour cream. Add to the processor and pulse until a cohesive dough is formed. If after a minute or so the mixture is still crumbly, add a few teaspoons of water and pulse again.

⑥ Form the dough into a disk and wrap in plastic wrap. Refrigerate and allow to chill for at least an hour. (The dough can be made in advance and chilled or frozen for 1 month.)

⑥ Make the filling: Preheat the oven to 350°. In the bowl of a food processor, pulse the mushrooms until finely chopped.

(*Mushroom Squares continued*)

◐ Melt the butter in a large nonstick skillet. Add the onion and cook until translucent. Add the mushrooms and cook until dry.

◐ Combine all of the remaining filling ingredients in a large mixing bowl. Add the mushroom mixture; stir to combine. Add salt and pepper to taste.

◐ In a small bowl whisk together the egg and water for an egg wash.

◐ Divide the chilled dough into 4 equal parts. Work with only 1 part at a time, returning the remainder to the refrigerator. Roll ¼ of dough out to about ⅛-inch thick. Cut into 2- to 3-inch squares and brush edges with egg wash. Place a small spoonful of filling in the center of each square and pinch up the edges into a pyramid. Brush with egg wash. Repeat until all of the dough and filling are used.

◐ Bake on ungreased baking sheets in the oven for 20 to 30 minutes or until golden brown.

Olivata Spread

Yield: 1 *cup*

If you love olives, this is nectar from the gods. Try it as a dip with fresh vegetables or with crackers or breads. This mixture will last for up to six months if refrigerated. Store in an airtight container and pour a thin layer of good quality olive oil over the top to preserve freshness. Bring to room temperature to serve.

1	pound oil-cured black or green olives, pitted
2	cloves garlic, peeled and finely minced
1	teaspoon dried oregano and
½	teaspoon dried rosemary
	Or
1	teaspoon dried basil and
1	teaspoon dried thyme
	Juice from 1 lemon
	Fresh ground black pepper to taste

◐ Combine the olives with the garlic and herbs in the bowl of a food processor fitted with a metal blade. Pulse the mixture to a grainy puree.

◐ Season with lemon and pepper to taste. Pulse to blend. Serve with fresh vegetables or assorted bread and crackers.

Notes

Index

Index

Index

Index

Mill House Inn
33 North Main Street
East Hampton, NY 11937
Phone: (516) 324-9766
Fax: (516) 324-9793

Name _____

Address _____

City _____ State _____ Zip _____

Phone _____

If you wish cookbooks to be mailed to other addresses, please enclose additional names and addresses on a separate piece of paper.

To order additional copies of **Tasting the Hamptons**:

Please contact the **Mill House Inn** at (516) 324-9766 or mail in this form with credit card information or a check payable to **Mill House Inn**.

Total Order: _____ copies   @ $19.95 each _____

NY residents add 8.25% sales tax   @ $ 1.64 each _____

Shipping and Handling   @ $ 3.75 each _____

                                        Balance Due _____

❑ Visa   ❑ MasterCard

Card Number _____ Exp. _____

Signature _____

Mill House Inn
33 North Main Street
East Hampton, NY 11937
Phone: (516) 324-9766
Fax: (516) 324-9793

Name _____

Address _____

City _____ State _____ Zip _____

Phone _____

If you wish cookbooks to be mailed to other addresses, please enclose additional names and addresses on a separate piece of paper.

To order additional copies of **Tasting the Hamptons**:

Please contact the **Mill House Inn** at (516) 324-9766 or mail in this form with credit card information or a check payable to **Mill House Inn**.

Total Order: _____ copies   @ $19.95 each _____

NY residents add 8.25% sales tax   @ $ 1.64 each _____

Shipping and Handling   @ $ 3.75 each _____

                                        Balance Due _____

❑ Visa   ❑ MasterCard

Card Number _____ Exp. _____

Signature _____

Mill House Inn
33 North Main Street
East Hampton, NY 11937
Phone: (516) 324-9766
Fax: (516) 324-9793

Name _____

Address _____

City _____ State _____ Zip _____

Phone _____

If you wish cookbooks to be mailed to other addresses, please enclose additional names and addresses on a separate piece of paper.

To order additional copies of **Tasting the Hamptons**:

Please contact the **Mill House Inn** at (516) 324-9766 or mail in this form with credit card information or a check payable to **Mill House Inn**.

Total Order: _____ copies   @ $19.95 each _____

NY residents add 8.25% sales tax   @ $ 1.64 each _____

Shipping and Handling   @ $ 3.75 each _____

                                        Balance Due _____

❑ Visa   ❑ MasterCard

Card Number _____ Exp. _____

Signature _____

Mill House Inn
33 North Main Street
East Hampton, NY 11937
Phone: (516) 324-9766
Fax: (516) 324-9793

Name _____

Address _____

City _____ State _____ Zip _____

Phone _____

If you wish cookbooks to be mailed to other addresses, please enclose additional names and addresses on a separate piece of paper.

To order additional copies of **Tasting the Hamptons**:

Please contact the **Mill House Inn** at (516) 324-9766 or mail in this form with credit card information or a check payable to **Mill House Inn**.

Total Order: _____ copies   @ $19.95 each _____

NY residents add 8.25% sales tax   @ $ 1.64 each _____

Shipping and Handling   @ $ 3.75 each _____

                                        Balance Due _____

❑ Visa   ❑ MasterCard

Card Number _____ Exp. _____

Signature _____

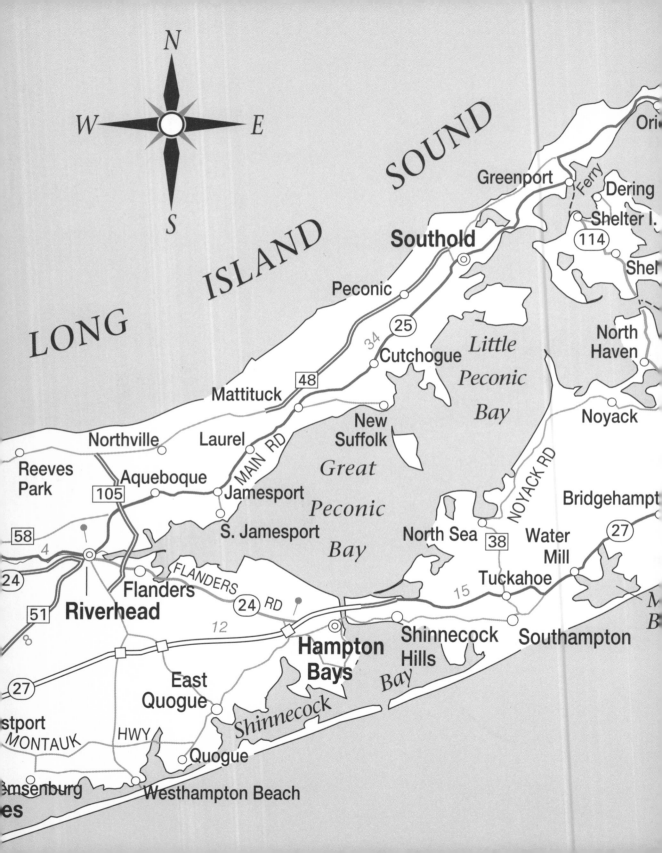